Training Guide

Sage Sterling +2 Financial Controller (for Windows)

Dexter J Booth

PITMAN
PUBLISHING

PITMAN PUBLISHING
128 Long Acre, London, WC2E 9AN

A Division of Longman Group UK Limited

First published in Great Britain 1993

British Library Cataloguing-in-Publication Data
A catalogue record for this book is available from the British Library.

ISBN 0 273 60468 6

Printed and bound in Great Britain by Clays Ltd, St Ives plc.

Contents

Introduction

The Sage Sterling +2 Financial Controller accounting system is a comprehensive integrated software package that permits you to keep a close and immediate control of your company accounts. This Guide is designed to introduce you to the package from the installation of the system onto your computer, through the basics of data entry to the generation of reports from your entered accounts. It is not intended that you will become competent in the intricacies of accountancy, but that you will learn how to handle the package in relation to your own book-keeping system. Indeed, there are certain aspects of account keeping that, because of the restricted size of the Guide, are necessarily treated in brief but which, in a real life situation, require more scope and depth. In particular, I refer to Task 37 which deals with VAT analysis. Only the most basic introduction is given and it is not intended that from this information you will be able to do more than use the package to produce a raw analysis. To produce an analysis that is usable for Customs and Excise purposes requires more knowledge of tax accounting than it is possible to give here.

This Guide follows from an earlier Guide that was written to introduce the first DOS version of the Financial Controller and in consequence, to enable updated users of that system who have already read the earlier Guide to compare the two systems, the scenario of the earlier Guide is retained.

Imagine that you are living on a remote Hebridean island and making a living by buying oysters and scallops and selling them to a variety of customers on the mainland. In addition, you buy firewood from the mainland and sell it to various people on the island. For some time your business has been developing, from small beginnings, but now you find that the market for your wares has increased sufficiently to warrant a capital injection from your private funds and a bank loan enabling you to expand the enterprise.

As you work your way through this Guide you will see the company develop and at the same time learn how the Sage Sterling +2 Financial Controller system can be used to keep a track of your affairs.

Getting started

The system The Sage Sterling +2 Financial Controller arrives at your door as a set of four diskettes, a User Guide and a booklet describing the EC VAT regulations. Each one of the diskettes contains the complete system and each is enclosed to cater for the type of computer system that you may have. The system can be installed onto your computer via a 5.25 or 3.5 inch disk drive to run either under DOS or Windows - hence the four diskettes.

In this Guide is is assumed that the Sage Sterling +2 Financial Controller system will be used to run from a hard disk under a previously installed 3.1 version of Windows. The system will run under Windows version 3.0 but, due to the inherent instability of Windows 3.0 when put under pressure, problems can arise. In addition, this Guide has been written using version 1.10A of the Sage Sterling +2 accounting system which contains the facility to generate remittance advices in contrast to version 1.10 which does not have that facility.

Installation It is assumed that if you need to install Sage Sterling +2 onto your computer then you already have Windows installed and that you are familiar with the Windows graphic user interface and the use of the mouse as a means of entering information into the computer.

To install Sage Sterling +2 for Windows execute the following procedure:

1 BOOT UP up your computer and ENTER **Windows.**

2 ENSURE that the **Windows Program Manager** window is on display.

3 PLACE the Sage Sterling +2 system diskette marked **PC Type WINDOWS** into the external drive A.

4 CLICK the **File** menu on the **Program Manager menu bar** to reveal a drop-down menu:

5 CLICK **Run...** to open the **Run** window.

6 In the dialog box of the **Run** window TYPE **A:INSTALL** and PRESS Enter.

This will activate the Sage Sterling +2 installation procedure which will display the **Financial Controller Install Program** window.

7 CLICK the **Install for the First Time** button and the contents of the **Financial Controller Install Program** window will change to a form requesting installation information which you will provide as follows:

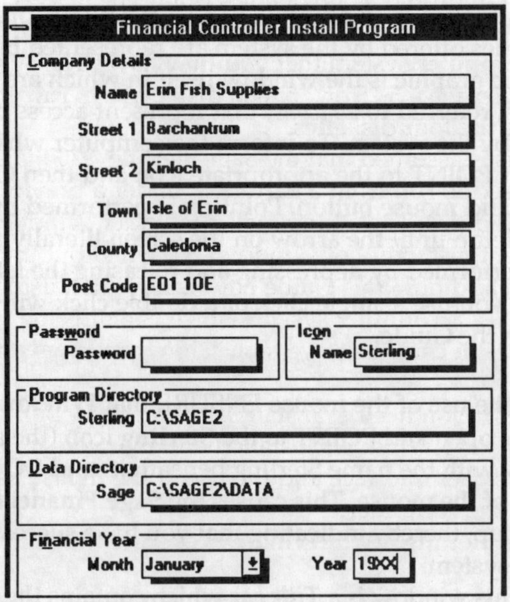

The **Password** dialog box has been left blank. If you wish to attach a password to your system this is where you do it. Then, every time you wish to enter the system from Windows you will be asked to provide the password.

The **Data Directory** path has, as default, C:\SAGE2 and this has been amended here to C:\SAGE2\DATA. Both directories SAGE2 and DATA will be created by Sage during the installation procedure.

The **Financial Year** has been set to start in January to avoid the system date falling outside the current financial year whenever dates are used in the Guide. The year is given here as 19XX as it is throughout the Guide. This is done to permit you to use the current year for all your data entries; REPLACE the XX with the particular year that is current as you read this Guide.

8 When you are satisfied that the form is correctly completed CLICK the **Install** button at the bottom of the window and the system will do the rest.

When the installation procedure is complete you will be so informed - again within the **Financial Controller Install Program** window.

9 CLICK the **Ok** button to close the window and to return to the **Program Manager** window of Windows where you will see a window called **Sage** on view in which is displayed two icons - the *Sterling* icon and the *Doctor* icon.

The Mouse

Because Sage Sterling +2 runs under Windows you will have to be familiar with the use of the mouse as a means of entering information into the computer and a brief outline is given here. For more detailed information, refer to your Windows manual.

The Windows system is an example of a *Graphics User Interface* (GUI) where the various facilities offered by the system are represented by pictures or *graphics*. The basic graphic is the window itself in which are contained a number of other graphics, referred to as *icons*, that represent access points to the facilities offered by the system. To inform the computer which facility you require you must POINT to the appropriate icon and then CLICK or DOUBLE CLICK the left-hand mouse button. Pointing is performed by moving the mouse around your tabletop until the arrow on the screen literally *points* at the graphic and clicking is performed by depressing and releasing the left-hand mouse button. Whether you use a single click or a double click will become clear as you progress through the Guide.

Entering Sage

To demonstrate the use of the mouse ENSURE that Windows is on display with the **Sage** window open and POINT to the **Sterling** icon (the small graphic inside the Sage window with the name Sterling beneath it) and DOUBLE CLICK the left-hand button of the mouse. This causes the **Sage Financial Controller** window to open up, thereby indicating that you have successfully accessed the Sage Sterling +2 system.

At the top of this window is a *Title bar* which contains the name of the window - in this case **Financial Controller**. At the right hand end of the **Title bar** is a box containing a downward pointing arrowhead. This box is called the *Minimize button* and can be used to shrink the window down to an icon. CLICK the **Minimize** button and you will see the effect - the **Financial Controller** window shrinks to its icon. DOUBLE CLICK the icon to retrieve the window.

POINT to the **Title bar**, depress and hold down the left-hand mouse button and then move the mouse over the tabletop. You will see the window move across the screen; this is known as DRAGGING. DRAG the window to the centre of the screen.

Behind the **Financial Controller** window is the **Windows Program Manager** window. CLICK the **Minimize** button on the **Windows Program Manager** window and instantly the **Program Manager** window shrinks to its icon leaving the **Financial Controller** window on display without all the background clutter.

To the immediate left of the **Title bar** is the *Control-menu* icon in the form of a small bar in a square box. This is your access point to exit from the Sage Sterling +2 system. DOUBLE CLICK the **Control-menu** icon and a window opens asking if you wish to backup your data. CLICK the **No** button and you will find that you have left Sage Sterling +2 system. DOUBLE CLICK the **Program Manager** icon to restore the **Program Manager** window.

Section A

Setting up the system

Task 1: The Financial Controller window
Task 2: Reviewing the ledger system
Task 3: The Nominal Ledger window
Task 4: Amending the nominal accounts structure
Task 5: Entering the startup capital and bank loan
Task 6: Setting up a supplier's details
Task 7: Entering a purchase invoice
Task 8: Paying a purchase invoice
Task 9: The transaction and control account histories
Task 10: The trial balance
Task 11: Journal entry of a van purchase
Task 12: Setting up the van loan prepayments
Task 13: Accounting for recurring entries
Task 14: Setting up asset depreciation

Task 1 The Financial Controller window

➤ **This Task will describe the Financial Controller window and demonstrate its status as a home base to all operations within the system.**

Enter the Sage Sterling +2 accounting system from Windows and display the **Financial Controller** window (REFER to *Getting Started*).

The **Financial Controller** window is your entry point into the Sage Sterling+2 accounting system. It is also the base from which you access all of the features that are available within the system.

As you will see, the window contains twelve buttons where each button serves as the entry point to a collection of facilities offered by the system - as described by the annotation on each button. For example:

Button	**Access**
Customers	Customer dealings and the Sales Ledger
Suppliers	Supplier dealings and the Purchase Ledger
Bank	Bank transactions

Activity 1.1 Entering the bank details

As an example of how different aspects of the **Financial Controller** are accessed via the buttons displayed in the **Financial Controller** window we shall access the **Bank Account** via the **Bank** button.

1 CLICK the **Bank** button to reveal the **Bank Accounts** window:

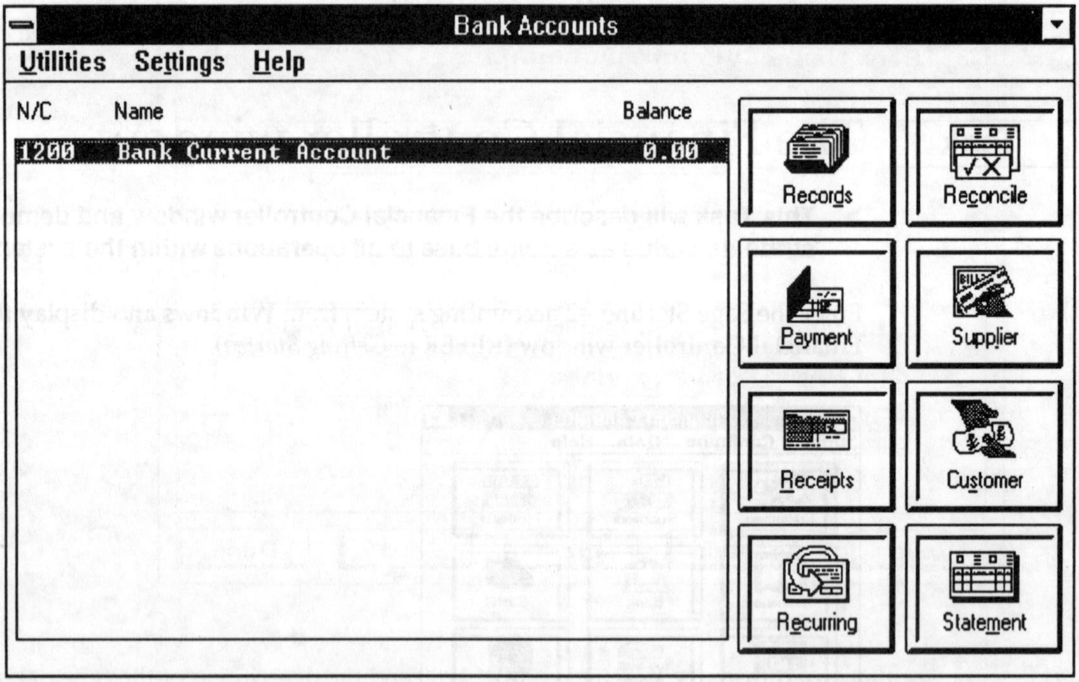

The **Bank Accounts** window has all the features common to other windows such as **Title bar, Control-menu box, Minimize** button and **Menu bar.** It also has a central area - an *information panel* - in which is displayed the nominal account codes that relate to the company's bank accounts, their names and their balances. Here you see that the company only has one bank account, namely, a current account and that it has the nominal code 1200 and a zero balance.

Down the right hand side of the **Bank Account** window you will see eight further buttons, the left-hand four of which are:

Button	**Permits**
Records	Access to the bank details
Payments	Payments out of the bank account to be recorded
Receipts	Payments into the bank account to be recorded
Recurring	Payments that are made regularly such as standing orders into and out of the bank account to be recorded

2 CLICK the **Records** button to reveal the **Bank Records** window.

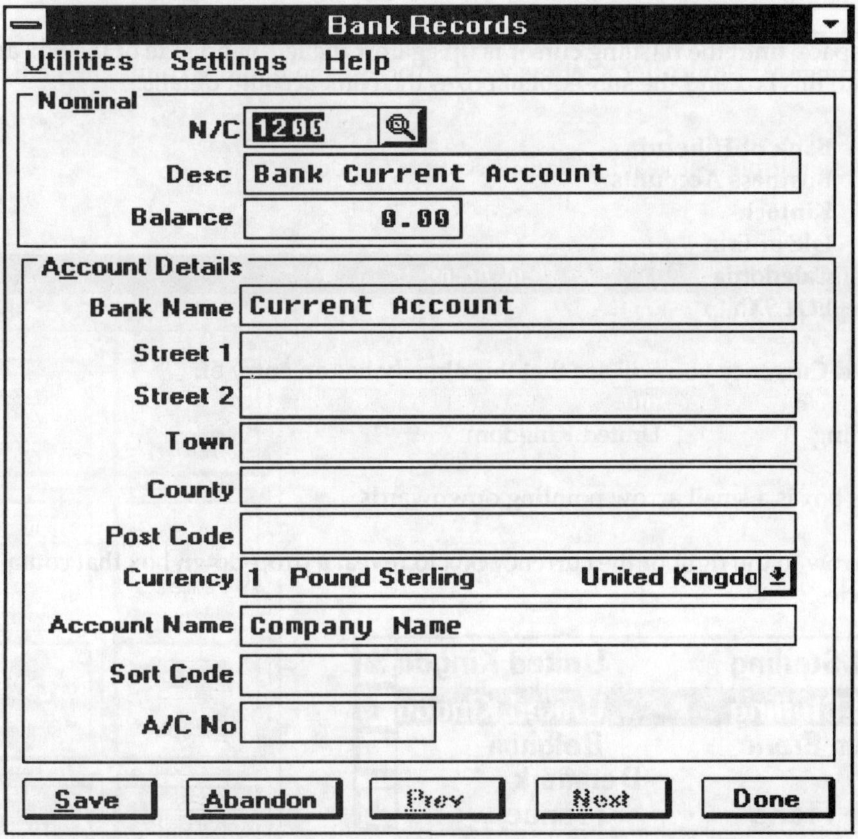

Here you see that, apart from the nominal code of 1200 and the description of the type of bank account, the system has no record of the bank details - it is up to you to provide them by typing them in. Notice that against the legend **Bank Name** is the phrase **Current Account**. We need to replace this phrase with the name of the bank.

3 POINT to immediate left of the word **Current** opposite **Bank Name** in the **Account Details** section of the window. As you point you will see that the arrow pointer changes to an I.

4 CLICK with the I to the left of Current. You will see a flashing line appear - this is called the cursor and if you were to start typing then this is where the type would appear.

5 HOLD DOWN the [Shift] key and then POINT and CLICK immediately to the right of the word **Current**. You will see the word **Current** become highlighted - you have now selected that word.

6 PRESS [Backspace] and the word **Current** disappears.

7 POINT to the word **Account** and DOUBLE CLICK. Again you will notice the word becomes highlighted. This is an alternative way to select a word.

8 PRESS [Backspace] and the word **Account** disappears leaving an empty box.

9 PRESS [Backspace] until the flashing cursor is up against the left-hand side of the box and then TYPE into this box and the subsequent boxes the bank account details:

Bank Name	**Bank of Hibernia**
Street1	**Business Accounts**
Street 2	**Kinloch**
Town	**Isle of Erin**
County	**Caledonia**
Post Code	**EO1 9XY**

At the box labelled **Currency** you will see that this already has an entry of:

1 Pound Sterling United Kingdom

At the side of this box is a small arrow pointing downwards.

10 CLICK the arrow to the right of the currency box to reveal a drop-down box that contains a list of currencies.

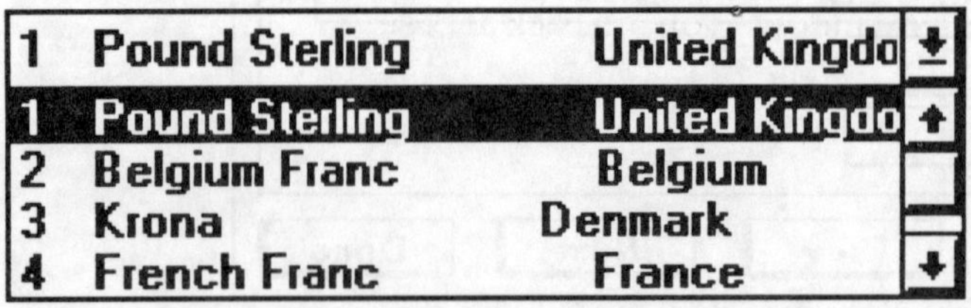

At the side of this window is a slider bar.

11 CLICK the arrow at the bottom of the slider bar and you will see the currencies scroll one currency per click.

12 When the currency **Guilder** appears CLICK the word **Guilder** and it will become highlighted and immediately entered as the **Currency** option in your bank account.

13 CHANGE the **Currency** option back to **Pounds Sterling**. You will have to CLICK the up arrow at the top of the slider bar until **Pounds Sterling** appears.

14 CONTINUE entering the following into the **Bank Records** window:

Account Name	**Erin Fish Supplies**
Sort Code	**01-02-03**
A/C No.	**90817263**

15 To complete this Activity and to ensure that these bank account details are recorded by the system CLICK the **Save** button located at the bottom of the window.

The bank details are then saved to disk. The details that you have just entered into the **Bank Record** window disappear to enable you to enter the details of another bank account. Notice that the **N/C** box is now empty.

No other bank account details are required.

16 DOUBLE CLICK the **Control-menu** box and the **Bank Records** window closes to reveal the **Bank Accounts** window.

17 As an alternative way to close a window PRESS Esc and the **Bank Accounts** window closes to reveal the **Financial Controller** window - you are back at base.

Task 2 Reviewing the ledger system

➤ **This task will demonstrate the central role played by the Nominal Ledger.**

Ensure that the **Financial Contoller** window is on display.

Three of the many facilities offered by the **Financial Controller** window are the three principal ledgers within the accounting system; the **Sales, Purchase** and **Nominal Ledgers** denoted by the **Customers, Suppliers** and **Nominal** buttons respectively.

Every company performs transactions with money and the purpose of the accounting system is to keep a record of both the transactions and the money associated with each transaction. This is done by assigning each transaction to an account and there are as many different accounts as there are different types of transaction. If the company buys a van to enable it to deliver its goods there may be a purchase account in the name of the company that sold the van and in that account will be recorded the amount paid for the van - in accounting terms it is said that the purchase invoice for the van will be *posted* to the **Purchase Ledger**. If the company sells a quantity of stock to a customer there will be a sales account in the name of the customer and all sales invoices to that customer will be posted to that account. If the company is registered for Value Added Tax (VAT) there will be a tax account in which all sales and purchases that involve tax will be posted, thereby recording all tax collected and all tax expenditure. The life history of every account is recorded in a *ledger* and to create order amongst the large variety of different accounts they are grouped into types. Because the principle aim of any company is to buy and sell, the two main ledgers are the *Sales Ledger* and the *Purchase Ledger*.

- **Sales Ledger**

All sales are recorded in the **Sales Ledger**, accessed via the **Customers** button, which contains a collection of sales accounts and the amounts of money each account owes the company.

- **Purchase Ledger**

All purchases are recorded in the **Purchase Ledger**, accessed via the **Suppliers** button, which contains a collection of purchase accounts and the amounts of money each account is owed by the company.

- **Nominal Ledger**

The **Nominal Ledger**, accessed via the **Nominal** button, records every transaction that the company makes. Every sale recorded in the **Sales Ledger** is also recorded in the **Nominal Ledger**, as is every purchase. Many accounts involve transactions that are neither sales nor purchases. For example, bank account transactions involve the payment in and the withdrawal out of money. Such transactions may be caused by a sale or a purchase but the transaction itself is neither a sale nor a purchase. This type of transaction is also recorded in the **Nominal Ledger**. As a consequence the **Nominal Ledger** contains the complete transaction life history of the company and as such plays a central role in the company's accounting system.

Because the **Nominal Ledger** stands between the *debtors* in the **Sales Ledger** and the *creditors* in the **Purchase Ledger** it has to keep a balance between the two. This is achieved by a system known as *double entry* book-keeping. In the ledgers, every recorded debit in one account is balanced by a credit of an equal amount in another account and vice versa. As a consequence, posting transactions to the **Nominal Ledger** has to be performed with great care to ensure that the balance is maintained. Fortunately, within the Sage Sterling+2 Financial Controller accounting system, sales and purchase transactions that are posted into the **Sales** and **Purchase Ledgers** are automatically posted into the **Nominal Ledger** via the various *control accounts* - we shall see later what these are.

Task 3 The Nominal Ledger window

➤ **This Task will view the facilities offered by the Nominal Ledger and display the account codes used by the Nominal Ledger.**

From the **Financial Controller** window CLICK the **Nominal** button. This will cause the **Nominal Ledger** window to be displayed.

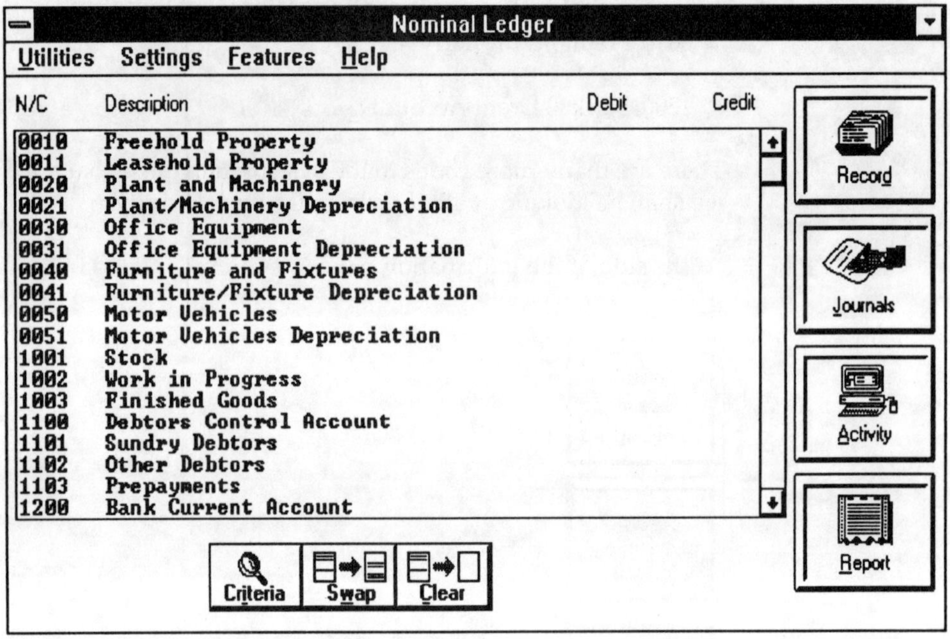

This screen is typical of all such screens within the system. There is a **Title bar** to tell you which window you are looking at. Just below the **Title bar** is a **Menu bar** containing four words:

These words represent menus of further options that relate to aspects of the system other than those contained within the **Nominal Ledger**. These options can be accessed simply by clicking the appropriate word. For example, CLICK the word **Utilities** and the following drop-down menu appears:

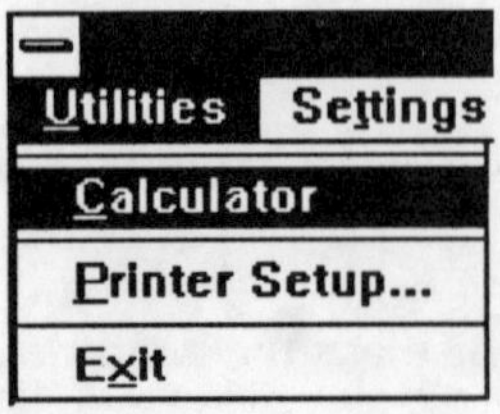

The dots after **Printer Setup** indicate that if this option is selected then you will be faced with further choices. For now, CLICK the word **Exit** and immediately you exit from the **Nominal Ledger** window and return to the **Financial Controller** window.

CLICK the **Nominal** button to return to the **Nominal Ledger** window.

Beneath the **Menu bar** you will see an information panel in which there is a list of **Nominal Ledger** account codes and their names, ranging from:

0010 Freehold Property

to

1200 Bank Current Account

There are many more codes in the system than those that are displayed here and we shall be looking at all of them in the next Activity.

At the side of the information panel are four annotated buttons:

These four buttons permit access to facilities that are related to the **Nominal Ledger**.

Activity 3.1 Viewing the Nominal Ledger Account Codes

1 CLICK the **Report** button at the bottom right-hand side of the **Nominal Ledger** window to reveal the **Nominal Ledger Reports** window.

In the centre of this window is an information panel that displays the **Nominal Ledger** codes and names and now you will see that the list extends to:

2102 Other Creditors

At the side of the information panel is a slider bar.

2 CLICK the down arrow at the bottom of the slider bar and you will notice that the list moves up one code per click.

3 CLICK inside the slider bar, below the slider and you will notice that the list now scrolls up a panel at a time.

4 CLICK inside the slider bar, above the slider and you will see the list scroll in the opposite direction.

5 CLICK the up arrow at the top of the slider bar and you will see the list scroll one code at a time.

6 DRAG the slider down and you will see the account descriptions move at the same time. Release the slider and the section of the list appropriate to that position of the slider is displayed.

By now you will realise that there is a large number of nominal accounts - the highest code being 9999 for the Mispostings Account.

Reports

A report gathers together a collection of accounts and their details according to some specified criteria or conditions. The specific accounts that are gathered and the details that are reported upon are first defined by using the facilities available in this window. Once the report has been so defined it is designated inside the **Output** box to be output either on the screen (**Display**) or at the printer (**Printer**).

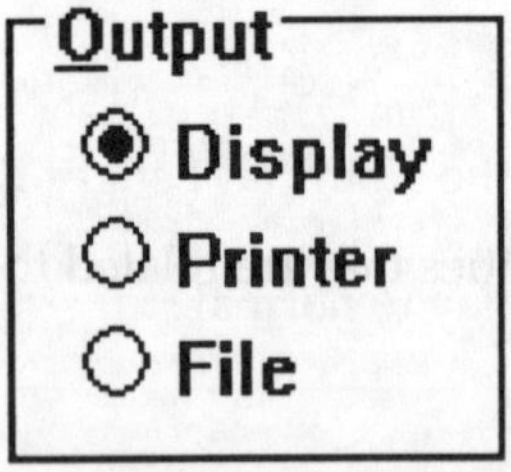

A third option (**File**) permits the report to be sent to a disk file for access at a later time. The activation of the report is governed by the collection of five buttons to the right of the window. The box labelled **Files** contains the names of those reports that have already been defined. As you will see, there are two reports that come with the system, namely Activity and Balances.

Activity 3.2 Reviewing the reporting facility of the Nominal Ledger

1 CLICK the word **Balances** in the **File** box to the top right of the **Nominal Ledger Reports** window. You will see it become highlighted in *reverse video* to indicate that it has been selected.

2 CLICK the **Display** radio button in the **Output** box to the bottom right of the **Nominal Ledger Reports** window to ensure that the report will be sent to the monitor screen.

3 CLICK the **Run** button to the right of the **Nominal Ledger Reports** window.

After a few moments a window called **File View** opens in which is displayed a report showing a 0.00 debit to every nominal ledger account. Use the slider bar at the side of the report to view as many of the nominal ledger codes as you wish. When you are satisfied that you have seen enough:

4 DOUBLE CLICK the **Control-menu** box at top left to return to close this window and return to the **Nominal Ledger Reports** window.

5 CLICK the slider bar at the side of the information panel until the account

0020 Plant and Machinery

comes into view.

6 CLICK the account description of account 0020 that is located in the information panel and you will see the account highlighted in *reverse video*.

7 RUN the report called **Activity** to be displayed on the screen and you will find a report of this single nominal account annotated with:

***** NO TRANSACTIONS *****

USE the slider bar at the bottom of the **File View** window to view all the details of this report.

8 DOUBLE CLICK the **Control-menu** box to return to the **Nominal Ledger Report** window.

9 CLICK the account description 0020 to return its display to normal.

Activity 3.3 To produce a printout of all the nominal codes

1 In the **Nominal Ledger Reports** window CLICK the **New** button to reveal the **Nominal Ledger Report Creation** window.

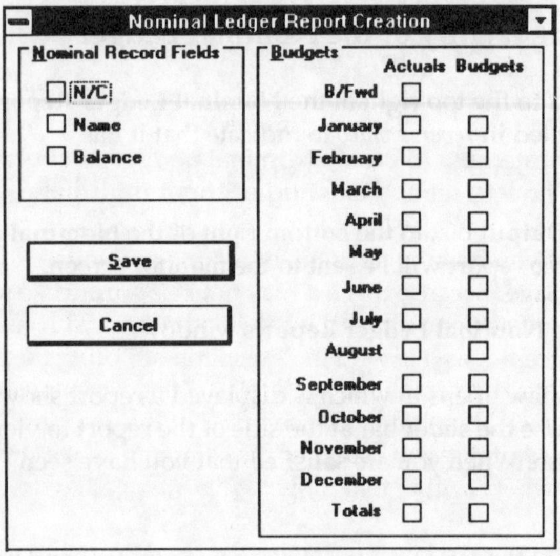

2 CLICK the box labelled N/C. A cross appears.

3 CLICK the box labelled Name. Another cross appears.

You have just instructed the system to create a report that contains just the nominal account codes and their names.

4 CLICK the **Save** button and in the **File Save As** window that appears TYPE the name of the report as LIST.

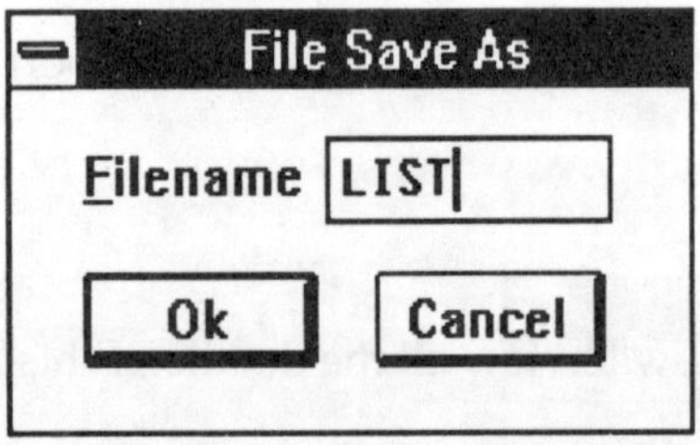

5 CLICK the **Ok** button and the report is saved to disk.
Notice that the new report called **list** appears highlighted in the **Files** box.

6 CLICK the **Printer** radio button to the bottom right of the **Nominal Ledger Reports** window.

7 CLICK the **Run** button and the report is sent to the printer - the complete list of nominal account codes and their names.

8 PRESS Esc twice in succession to return to the **Financial Controller** window.

Task 4 Amending the nominal accounts structure

➤ **This Task will demonstrate how to create Nominal Ledger account names and codes and how to amend existing account information.**

The nominal account list that you have just printed out in the previous Task is the default list provided by Sage. Because this list may not be appropriate to your existing company account structure it can be amended to suit your needs. For our purposes we shall accept it as it is with the exception of noting that it has no account dealing with the startup capital required to start the company. We shall rectify this by creating such an account. Notice first that the accounts in the range 3000 to 3999 cover the capitalisation aspect of the company so we should place our new account somewhere within that range. What we need to do is to look at the range

From the **Financial Controller** window CLICK the **Nominal** button to reveal the **Nominal Ledger** window. At the bottom of the window are three buttons:

These three buttons deal with the facility of selecting specific accounts from the **Nominal Ledger.**

Activity 4.1 Selecting accounts by criteria

1 CLICK the **Criteria** button to reveal the **Nominal Account List Criteria** window.

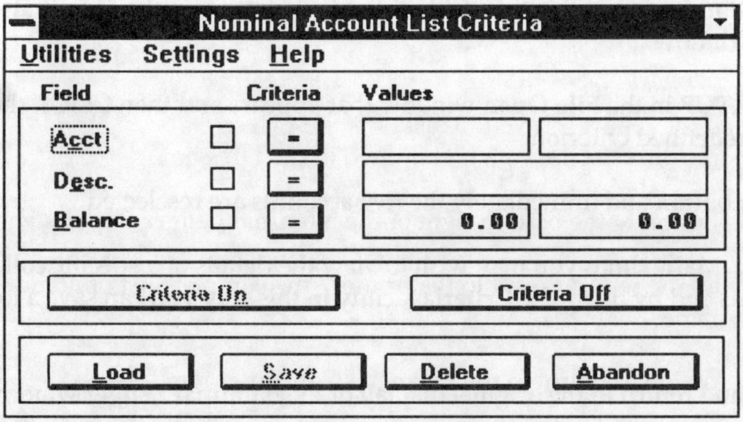

2 CLICK the square box to the right of **Acct**.

3 CLICK the button to the immediate right of this square (labelled =) four times until it displays <>.

4 Under the heading **Values**, ENTER the number **3000** into the first box and **3999** into the second box to the right of the first.

The symbol <> stands for *between the values* and what you have entered here is an instruction to the system to identify those Nominal Ledger codes between the values 3000 and 3999 inclusive.

5 CLICK the **Criteria On** button and the **Nominal Account List Criteria** window disappears to reveal the information panel of the **Nominal Ledger** window displaying just the five accounts:

3000	Ordinary Shares
3001	Preference Shares
3100	Reserves
3101	Undistributed Reserves
3200	Profit and Loss Account

You decide from the information displayed here that the new account will have the number 3102. Notice that the **Criteria** button now has the word **ON** displayed in the middle telling you that a selection criterion is in force.

6 CLICK the **Criteria** button to re-display the **Nominal Account List Criteria** window.

7 CLICK the **Save** button and at the prompt in the **File Save As** window TYPE the name of the criterion as **STARTUP**.

8 CLICK the **Ok** button to save the file to disc.

9 CLICK the **Criteria Off** button to return the **Nominal Ledger** information panel display to its original state.

10 CLICK the **Criteria** button again but this time CLICK the **Load** button in the **Nominal Account List Criteria** window.

11 CLICK the word **STARTUP** in the **File Open** window that appears and then CLICK the **Ok** button to load in the predefined criterion.

12 CLICK the **Criteria On** button and immediately the five accounts are reselected.

This is a most useful device. Many times you may wish to view the details of a specific collection of **Nominal Ledger** accounts and by using the **Criteria** facility in this way you can save a lot of time accessing them.

13 TURN the **Criteria** off and return to the original display of the **Nominal Ledger** window.

Activity 4.2 Selecting accounts individually

Ensure that the **Nominal Ledger** window is on display with the accounts visible in the information panel.

1 CLICK any account description and you will see the description highlighted in *reverse video* to indicate that it has been selected.

2 CLICK any other account and you will see that selected as well.

3 CLICK the **Swap** button and you will see the highlight reverse - the two accounts selected are deselected and the accounts that were not selected are selected in their stead. CLICK the **Swap** button repeatedly to see its effect.

4 CLICK the **Clear** button to return the display to its original state.

Activity 4.3 Adding a Nominal Ledger account

Ensure that the **Nominal Ledger** window is on display with no accounts selected.

1 CLICK the **Record** button to reveal the **Nominal Ledger Record** window.

2 TYPE the number **3102** in the box labelled **N/C** - this is the number of the new nominal ledger account.

3 CLICK the **Name** box and the legend *** New Account *** appears.

4 TYPE **Startup Capital** in the box called **Name**.

You have entered sufficient information to create this new account. Now it must be stored by the system.

5 CLICK the **Save** button.
The details of this new account are saved to disk and the information you just entered disappears leaving a blank **Nominal Ledger Record**.

6 CLICK the **Done** button or PRESS [Esc] to close the **Nominal Ledger Record** window.

You have now created a new **Nominal Ledger** account number 3102 and two clicks of the slider bar will display it in the information panel.

Activity 4.4 Amending an existing account

The nominal account **Bad Debt Write-Off** has code 8100. You are going to set aside £3000 in this account to cater for any bad debts that may occur. This will mean retaining the Account Reference and Account Name but amending the Yearly Budget from the default of 0.00 to 3000.00. From the **Nominal Ledger** window CLICK the slider bar *or* DRAG the slider until the account 8100 **Bad Debt Write-Off** appears.

1 CLICK the code **8100** in the information panel to highlight it and thereby select it.

2 CLICK the **Record** button and the **Nominal Ledger Record** of account 8100 appears automatically.

3 CLICK the box labelled **Totals** at the foot of the centre column headed **Budgets** and the flashing cursor will appear there.

4 TYPE in the number **3000**.

5 CLICK any other box. Immediately all the monthly budget boxes display the value 250.00 - the monthly budget which, over the twelve months of the year, totals 3000.

6 CLICK the **Save** box and PRESS [Esc] to store the information and then close the window.

Activity 4.5 View the new accounts

From the **Nominal Ledger** window use the scroll bar to scroll the display of accounts. When you are satisfied that the new account number 3102 has been posted correctly run off a new printed copy of the amended account codes. It is always useful to have a printed copy at hand when posting transactions to the ledgers. When the printing is complete PRESS [Esc] to return to the **Financial Controller** window.

Task 5 Entering the startup capital and bank loan

➤ **This Task illustrates the use of nominal ledger codes and the posting of bank receipts into the ledger.**

You are now ready to start setting up the ledger system for your company, Erin Fish Supplies. From the **Financial Controller** window CLICK the **Bank** button to display the **Bank Accounts** window.

Activity 5.1 Entering the formation capital Bank Receipt

1 CLICK the **Receipts** button to reveal the **Bank Receipts** window containing a form entitled **Bank Current Account.**

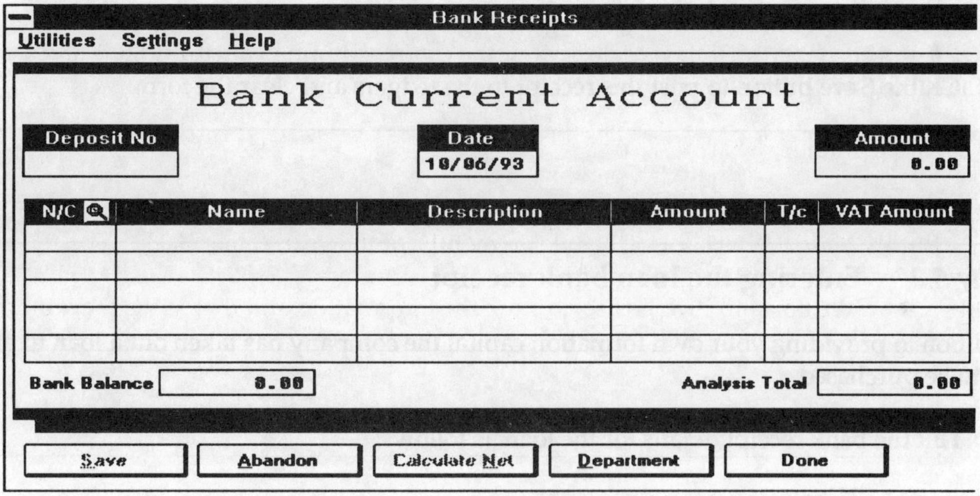

2 ENTER the following information into this screen:

Deposit No	1	
Date	01/08/XX	1 August 19XX. (The default here is the current date - you will have to change it and *remember* the XX must be substituted with your current year.)

3 CLICK the N/C box.

When posting transactions to ledgers it is necessary to have at hand a list of the **Nominal Ledger** account codes. If, however, you have temporarily mislaid your printed copy Sage has provided a useful facility of allowing you to view them via the **Finder** (denoted by the spy glass).

4 CLICK the **Finder** (spy glass) and there will be displayed a window containing the account names and codes. CLICK the slider bar until the code **3102 Startup Capital** appears in the list.

5 CLICK the account description to highlight it.
PRESS [Enter] *or* CLICK the **Ok** button and the account code number is automatically entered into the **Bank Current Account** form and the account name **Startup Capital** is entered beneath **Name**. Alternatively you could have just typed the number in.

6 COMPLETE the screen entry as follows:

Description	**Formation Capital**	
Amount	**12000.00**	
T/c	**T9**	This is the VAT tax code for a non-rated item.
VAT Amount	**0.00**	There is no tax paid so the system calculates this to be zero.

7 CLICK the **VAT Amount** box to ensure a display of 0.00.
Notice that the **Amount** box at the top right of this form contains the number 12000.00 in agreement with the **Analysis Total** at the bottom of the form. Notice that the **Bank Balance** at the bottom left of this form is also registering the 12000.00.

8 CLICK the **Save** button to post this receipt to the ledgers and clear the form.

Activity 5.2 Entering the loan bank receipt

In addition to providing your own formation capital the company has taken out a loan to enable a van to be purchased.

1 ENTER the bank receipt details for the loan as follows:

Deposit No	**2**	
Date	**01/08/XX**	Substitute the XX with your current year
Amount		Leave blank
N/C	**2300**	Use the **Finder**

Notice that the **N/C Name** now displays **Loans**.

Description	**Bank Loan**
Amount	**7000.00**
T/c	**T9**
VAT Amount	**0.00**

Notice that the **Amount** box at the top of the form has been filled in automatically with the correct amount.

2 CLICK the **Save** button to post this receipt to the ledgers.

3 CLICK the **Done** button to close the window.

Notice that from the information panel of the **Bank Accounts** window you will see the balance of the **Bank Current Account** at 19000.00 - the sum of the two receipts just posted.

4 PRESS [Esc] to return to the **Financial Controller** window.

Accounting performed:

The Bank Current Account is *debited* by the gross amount (untaxed value plus tax).
The Nominal Income accounts 2300 and 3102 are *credited* by the appropriate untaxed net amounts.

Had there been a tax amount then this would have been posted to a **VAT Control Account.**

Task 6 Setting up a supplier's details

➤ **In this Task you will learn how to enter a supplier's name and address and account details into the system.**

You now have £19,000 in the bank and you need to purchase a refrigeration unit in which to keep your stock. This is a purchase and so the transaction will be recorded in the **Purchase Ledger**. Before we can enter a transaction into this ledger we must create a **purchase ledger** account for the supplier of the refrigeration unit.

Starting from the **Financial Controller** window CLICK the **Suppliers** button to display the **Suppliers** window:

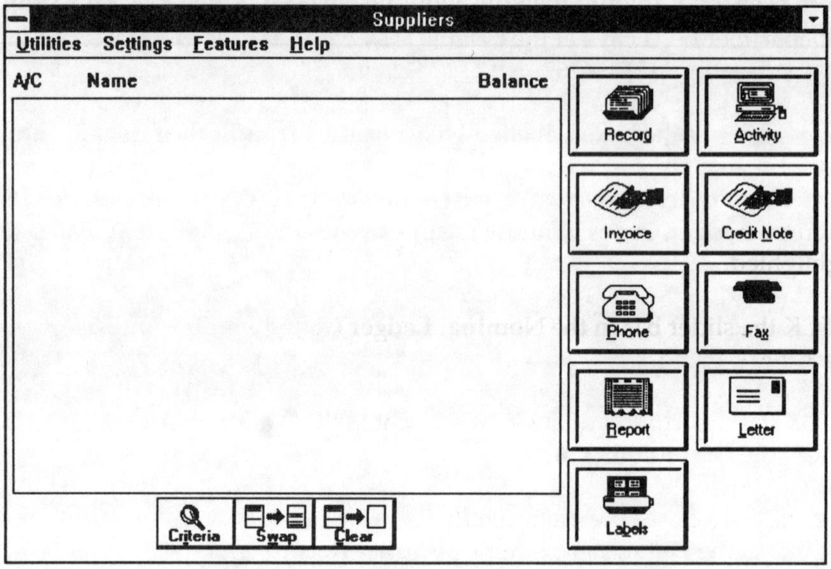

Activity 6.1 Entering supplier details

From the **Suppliers** window:

1 CLICK the **Record** button to reveal the **Supplier Record** window and ENTER the account name as **FRIDGE**.

A/C **FRIDGE**

This is the **Purchase Ledger** equivalent of a **Nominal Ledger** code. Such codes are not restricted to being numbers but can be a mixture of numbers and letters. When you have typed this entry CLICK the **Name** box causing the legend *** New Account *** to appear.

2 ENTER the following into the rest of the screen:

Name	**ColdWare Ltd**
Street 1	**123 Ice Palace Road**
Street 2	
Town	**Bergton**
County	
Post Code	**BE1 1EB**
Contact	**Jack Frost**
Telephone	**0123 456789**
Fax	
Analysis 1	
Analysis 2	
Analysis 3	
Department	**(Leave at the default 1, Department 1 is to be reserved for purchases)**
Tax ID	**123456789**

Leave the entries in the boxes labelled **History** and **Terms** as their default values.

3 CLICK the **Finder** spyglass to the right of **Nominal 5000** in the **Defaults** box, causing the **Nominal Ledger Codes** window to appear with the account **5000 Materials Purchases** highlighted.

4 CLICK the slider bar in the **Nominal Ledger Codes** window until account **0020 Plant and Machinery** appears.

5 CLICK the description of the 0020 account in the **Nominal Ledger Codes** window and then CLICK the **Ok** button.

This immediately closes the **Nominal Ledger Codes** window and replaces the nominal code 5000 to 0020 in the **Defaults** box in the **Supplier Record** window.

6 LEAVE the Tax Code entry as the default T1.

7 When you are satisfied that the details entered are correct CLICK the **Save** button to save the details and then CLICK the **Done** button to close the window and to return to the **Suppliers** window where you will see the **Purchase Ledger** account FRIDGE listed in the information panel.

Task 7 Entering a purchase invoice

➤ **In this Task you will learn how to post a purchase invoice into the Purchase Ledger.**

Having established a supplier account we can now record transactions between the company and the supplier in that account. The company has purchased a refrigeration unit from ColdWare Ltd at a cost of £3,600 plus VAT and a purchase invoice has been received from them. The details of this purchase invoice must now be posted into the **Purchase Ledger.**

Activity 7.1 Entering the purchase invoice details

From the **Suppliers** window:

1 CLICK the supplier description of the FRIDGE account as displayed in the information panel. The description will then become highlighted in *reverse video* to indicate that it has been selected.

2 CLICK the **Invoice** button to reveal the **Suppliers** window in which is displayed the **Supplier Invoice** form with the A/C and Name already entered.

3 COMPLETE the entry as follows:

Date	**01/08/XX**	*Remember,* substitute the current year for XX
Ref	**773**	This happens to be ColdWare's invoice number
N/C	**0020**	Use the **Finder**

The **Nominal Account** name appears automatically.

4 CONTINUE entering the invoice details

Description	**Refrigeration unit**	
Amount	**3600**	
T/C	**T1**	This is the default value as picked from ColdWare's record created in the previous Task

5 CLICK the **VAT Amount** box and the tax amount of 630.00 is displayed along with the invoice total of 4230.00.

6 CLICK the **Save** button to post the details to the ledgers.

7 PRESS [Esc] twice in succession to return to the **Financial Controller** window.

Accounting performed:

The Creditor's Control Account is *credited* with the gross amount.
The Nominal Account 0020 is *debited* with the net amount.
The Tax Control Account is *debited* with the tax amount.

Task 8 Paying a purchase invoice

➤ **In this Task you will learn how to pay an invoice and how to post a purchase invoice payment into the system.**

The refrigeration unit was purchased from ColdWare without any credit arrangements and so the purchase invoice was paid when the unit was delivered. We must now post this payment into the **Purchase Ledger**. From the **Financial Controller** window CLICK the **Bank** button to display the **Bank Accounts** window.

Activity 8.1 Posting the purchase invoice payment

From the **Bank Accounts** window CLICK the **Supplier** button to display the **Supplier Cheque** window which shows a blank cheque in the top half of the window and a ledger posting form in the bottom half.

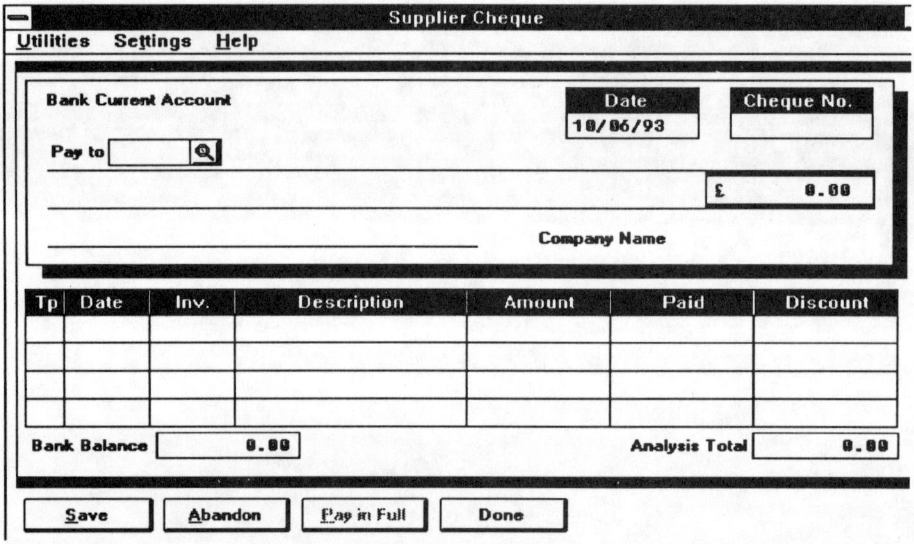

1 CLICK the **Finder** on the cheque **Pay to** box to reveal the **Supplier Accounts** window with the single account FRIDGE selected.

2 CLICK the **Ok** button to close the window and automatically enter the details of the outstanding purchase invoice into the **Supplier Cheque** window and the ledger posting form.

3 CHANGE the date to **01/08/XX** and ENTER the Cheque No. as **1**.

4 CHECK the entered details in the ledger posting form are as they should be:

TP	**PI**	Type of transaction is a Purchase Invoice
Date	**0108XX**	The XX will be substituted with your current year
Inv	**773**	This is the supplier's invoice number
Description	**Refrigeration unit**	
Amount	**4230.00**	

5 When you are satisfied that all the details are correctly entered LOOK at the buttons at the bottom of the form.

The faint printing on the **Pay in Full** button indicates that this button cannot be activated. CLICK the **Pay in Full** button to see the lack of effect.

6 CLICK the **Paid** box on the ledger posting form which is currently reading 0.00. When you have done this the printing on the **Pay in Full** button becomes darker indicating that it is now available to be activated.

7 CLICK the **Pay in Full** button and the cheque details are automatically completed as well as those on the entry form below.

8 CLICK the **Save** button to post the details to the ledgers.

9 CLICK the **Done** button and you are returned to the **Bank Accounts** window with the **Bank Current Account** displaying a balance of £14770.00 which is the difference between the £19000.00 paid in and the £4230.00 paid out.

10 PRESS [Esc] to return to the **Financial Controller** window.

Accounting performed:

The Creditor's Control Account is *debited* with the payment.
The Bank Account is *credited* with the payment.

Task 9 The transaction and control account histories

➤ **This Task describe some of the standard reporting facilities offered by the system.**

From the **Financial Controller** window CLICK the **Nominal** button.

Activity 9.1 Viewing the Transaction History in the Nominal Ledger

1 From the **Nominal Ledger** window use the slider bar to view all those accounts with a non-zero debit or credit and CLICK the description of each one in turn (there are just five of them).

2 CLICK the **Activity** button and the transactions will now be displayed in the **Nominal Ledger Transaction History** window for each nominal account reference code at a time.

The first transaction to be displayed is the transaction entered into the system of the purchase invoice for the refrigeration unit with **Nominal Account** code 0020. Beneath the heading **Tp** (Type of transaction) are the letters **PI**. These refer to the type of transaction being a Purchase Invoice.

3 CLICK the down arrow at the end of the **Acct bar** to reveal a drop-down box containing the names and account numbers of all those accounts selected.

4 CLICK the account **2300 Loans** and the **Nominal Ledger Transaction History** display changes to the **Bank Loan.**

5 REPEAT this procedure to view the account **3102 Startup Capital.**

6 PRESS Esc to exit the **Nominal Ledger Transaction History** window and return to the **Nominal Ledger** window.

Activity 9.2 Viewing the bank account history

1 From the **Nominal Ledger** window CLICK the **Clear** button to clear all the previous selections.

2 CLICK the account **1200 Bank Current Account.**

3 CLICK the **Activity** button and the display shows the three bank transactions with a final balance in the bank of £14,770.00.

Under **Tp** (for *type* of transaction) you will see **BR** and **PP**. These stand for Bank Receipt and Purchase Payment respectively.

No.	Tp	Date	Ref	Details	Value	Debit	Credit
1	BR	0108XX	1	Formation Capital	12000.00	12000.00	
2	BR	0108XX	2	Bank loan	7000.00	7000.00	
4	PP	0108XX	FRIDGE	Supplier Payment	4230.00		4230.00
				Totals		19000.00	4230.00
				Balance		14770.00	

Notice that payment into the bank is recorded as a debit to the bank account and payment out as a credit to the bank account.

4 When you feel that you appreciate all the information displayed on this screen PRESS Esc to return to the **Nominal Ledger** window.

5 CLICK the **Clear** button to clear the selected account.

Activity 9.3 Viewing the Creditor's Control Account

1 From the **Nominal Ledger** window CLICK **2100 Creditor's Control Account.**

2 CLICK the **Activity** button to reveal the **Nominal Ledger Transaction History** window where you will see the value of the refrigeration unit (the gross amount paid for it) as a credit to the account and the actual payment for the unit as a debit to the account. Notice that the credit balances the debit as shown by the Balance figure of 0.00.

3 When you feel that you appreciate all the information displayed on this screen PRESS Esc twice to return to the **Financial Controller** window.

Task 10 The trial balance

➤ **This Task demonstrates how to obtain a Trial Balance.**

The **Trial Balance** facility provides a check that the nominal accounts do balance. Ensure that the **Financial Controller** window is on display.

Activity 10.1 Viewing the Trial Balance

1 From the **Financial Controller** window CLICK the **Financials** button to reveal the **Financials** window:

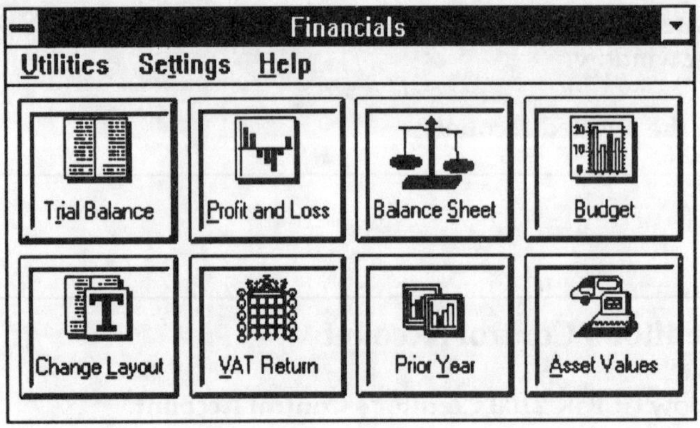

2 CLICK the **Trial Balance** button to reveal the **Nominal Ledger Trial Balance** window in which is displayed the current state of the company.

N/C	Name	Debit	Credit
0020	Plant & Machinery	3600.00	
1200	Bank Current Account	14770.00	
2201	Purchase Tax Control Account	630.00	
2300	Loans		7000.00
3102	Startup Capital		12000.00

At the bottom of the screen the totals are displayed:

		19000.00	19000.00

which shows that the debits balance the credits.

3 PRESS Esc twice to return to the **Financial Controller** window.

Task 11 Journal entry of a van purchase

➤ **This Task demonstrates how to enter a purchase and payment into the Nominal Ledger without using the Purchase Ledger.**

Your company has bought a van to enable deliveries to be made. This was bought on the mainland from a second-hand car dealer with a servicing agreement. After the service you will probably never have any further dealings with that company so there is no need to set up a purchase account for it. The purchase and payment transactions must however, be posted to the **Nominal Ledger**. Because you will not be posting via the **Purchase Ledger** you will have to post directly into the **Nominal Ledger**. Such postings are called *journal entries* and must be performed with caution as any posting to the **Nominal Ledger** must have a balancing debit and credit. Ordinarily, when posting via the **Purchase Ledger** such balancing is performed by the control accounts and you need not concern yourself with the intricacies. However, when posting directly into the **Nominal Ledger** it is best to write out the posting on a sheet of paper first.

Activity 11.1 Preparing for a Journal Entry

1 From the **Financial Controller** window CLICK the **Nominal** button to display the **Nominal Ledger** window.

The company has purchased a van costing £8000 plus VAT at 17.5%, giving a total payment of:

£8000 + £1400 = £9400

You might check this figure using the calculator.

2 CLICK the word **Utilities** on the **Menu bar** to reveal a drop-down menu.

3 CLICK the word **Calculator** and the **Windows calculator** appears.

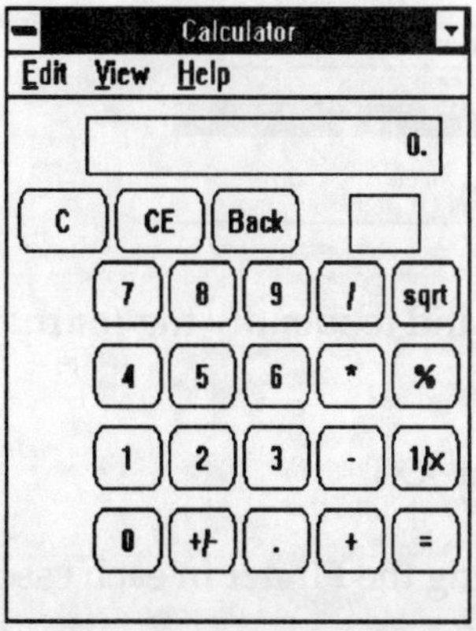

4 TYPE the number **8000** and you will see it appear in the calculator window.

5 TYPE * for multiplication followed by **1.175** and then **=**.
The display then shows the correct result as 9400.

6 DOUBLE CLICK the **Calculator Control-menu bar** to remove the calculator.

Having checked the total cost of the van, this purchase must be entered as:

£9400 Credit Nominal Code 1200 for Bank Current Account
£8000 Debit Nominal Code 0050 for Motor Vehicles
£1400 Debit Nominal Code 2201 for Purchase Tax Control Account

You are now ready to post these details as a **Journal Entry**.

Activity 11.2 Making a Journal Entry

1 With the **Nominal Ledger** window on display CLICK the **Journals** button to reveal the **Nominal Ledger Transaction** window containing a **Journal Entry** form.

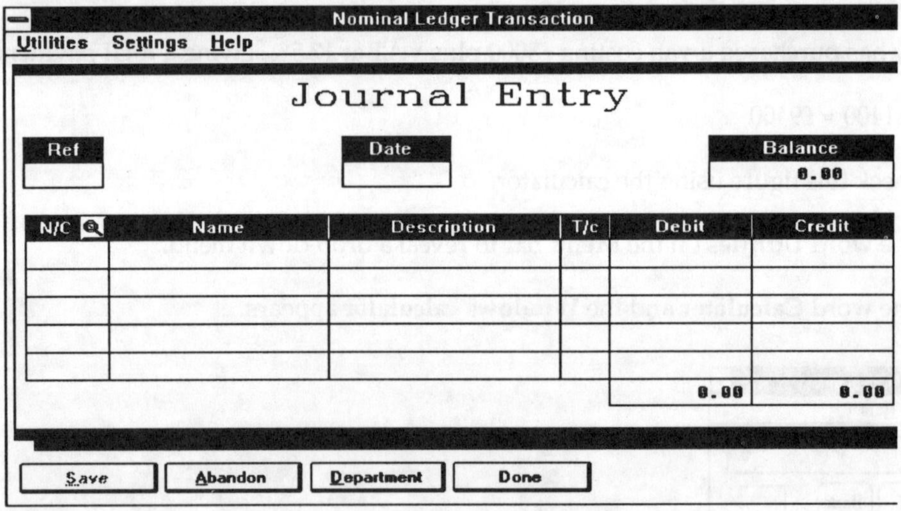

2 Under **Ref** TYPE in **VANPUR** to represent the van purchase and to identify the **Journal Entry**.

3 TYPE in the Date as **01/08/XX** (Substitute your current year for XX).

4 ENTER the debit and credit as described in the following, using the **Finder** in each case:

N/C	Name	Description	T/c	Debit	Credit
1200	Bank Current Account	Van Purchase	T9		**9400.00**
0050	Motor Vehicles	Untaxed van	T1	**8000.00**	
2201	Purchase Tax Control	Tax paid for van	T1	**1400.00**	

Notice the nominal account code 2201. This is reserved for VAT paid during a purchase and must be used whenever tax is entered in this way.

When you have completed the entry notice that the balance is zero. This means that the **Nominal Ledger** entry that you are proposing to make does indeed balance because the two Debit values add up to the credit value. If it did not balance then the system would not let you make the posting.

5 CLICK the **Save** button to save the posting to disk.

6 PRESS [Esc] to close the window and return to the **Nominal Ledger** window.

You may now wish to look through the Activity and Balances reports available from the **Nominal Ledger** screen to see the effect of the posting you have just made.

7 COMPLETE this Activity by displaying the **Financial Controller** window.

Task 12 Setting up the van loan prepayments

➤ **This Task demonstrates how to spread a one-off payment through the accounting year.**

Your arrangements with the bank when your company borrowed £7000 to enable it to buy a van was that the company would pay interest only at 18% for the full year and at the year end would pay off the outstanding loan amount of £7000. We shall consider the interest payments in the next Task and here we shall be concerned with the normal accounting practice of spreading a load. The outstanding amount of £7000 which is due to be paid in a year's time will be accounted for in twelve equal monthly installments each of which will be automatically posted to the **Nominal Ledger** every month as a prepayment during the month end procedure. The facility to set up prepayments and accruals is available from within the **Nominal Ledger** under **Prepayments and Accruals.**

From the **Financial Controller** window CLICK the **Nominal** button to display the **Nominal Ledger** window.

Activity 12.1 Setting up a prepayment

1 From the **Nominal Ledger** window CLICK the **Features** menu command to display a drop-down menu:

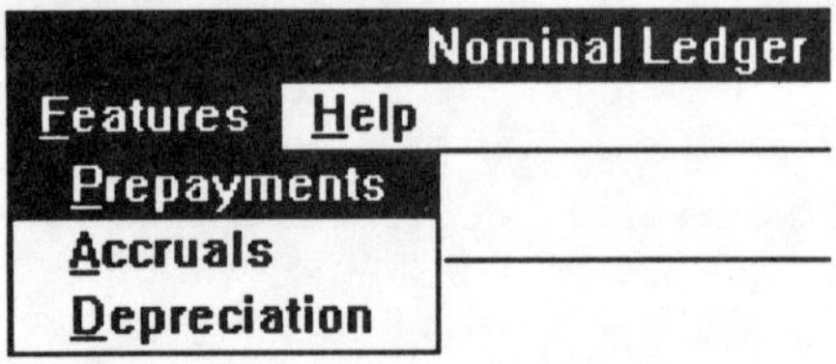

2 CLICK the **Prepayments** option to display a **Prepayments** form and enter the following details:

N/C	**2300**	the **Loans Nominal Ledger** code - you *must* use the **Finder** here to enter this code into the form
Description	**Van loan repayment**	
Value	**7000.00**	
Mth	**12**	spread over 12 months

3 CLICK the **N/C** box on the next line down and the Net Amount to be posted each month appears auotmatically as £583.33.

4 CLICK the **Save** button to save the details to disk and to return you to the **Nominal Ledger** window.

Activity 12.2 Setting up additional prepayments

In addition to the van loan repayment you will have other lump sums to pay for at other times during the year. Your total insurance commitment of £250 is due in six months' time and the company is committed to a van service in nine months' time that is set at £125, both items attracting VAT at the standard rate. Set up two more prepayments to spread this load - the first over six months and the second over nine months. Use **Nominal Ledger** codes 8204 for the Insurance; 7301 (Repairs and Servicing) for the van service and use the calculator to work out the totals due. For example, for the van service:

1 ENTER the van service prepayment details up to but excluding the value amount.

2 CLICK the **Value** box to ensure that the cursor is in that box.

3 REVEAL the **Calculator** using the **Utilities** command on the **Menu bar.**

4 ENTER the following

125 * 1.175 =

and the number 146.875 appears.

5 CLICK the **Edit** menu command in the **Calculator** window to reveal a drop-down menu containing the two words:

Copy
Paste

6 CLICK the command **Copy** in the drop-down menu.
The number in the **Calculator** display has now been copied onto the Windows' clipboard.

7 CLICK anywhere in the **Prepayments** window to bring it to the front and check that the cursor is still in the **Value** box.

8 PRESS [Shift-Ins] and the number 146.875 (which will eventually round to 146.88) appears in the **Value** box. The Shift-Ins command is Windows' Paste command and when issued will copy whatever is on the clipboard and paste it to wherever the cursor is located in the active window.

9 When you are satisfied that all three prepayments have been entered correctly, CLICK the **Save** button to save the information to disk.

At this stage you may feel that you have posted the van loan prepayment twice. This is not so because you have not even posted it once yet. The information contained on the **Prepayments** form is stored by the computer on the hard disk for posting to the ledgers at a later time during the month end procedures.

10 PRESS [Esc] to return to the **Financial Controller** window.

11 CLICK the **Calculator** window to bring it in the front of the **Financial Controller** window.

12 DOUBLE CLICK the **Calculator Control-menu** box to close the **Calculator** window.

Task 13 Accounting for recurring entries

➤ **This Task demonstrates how to set up recurring entries that are posted at the end of each month during the month end procedure.**

At 18% per annum the interest on the £7000 loan runs at £105 per month. It has been agreed to pay this by standing order and this recurring transaction must now be accounted for.

Activity 13.1 Setting up recurring entries for van loan interest

1 From the **Financial Controller** window CLICK the **Bank** button.

2 From the **Bank Accounts** window CLICK the **Recurring** button and enter the following details into the **Recurring Entries** form:

Tp	**BP**	Bank Payment
N/C	**7900**	Bank Interest Paid Nominal Account code (Use the **Finder**)
Date	**31/08/XX**	Enter the date when the first entry is to be posted during the month end procedures. The system will automatically update this date by a month at a time in readiness for subsequent postings.
Ref		Leave blank
Bank	**1200**	Use the **Finder**
Description	**Loan int**	
Net Amount	**105.00**	
T/c	**T9**	Bank interest is not rated for VAT and not rated items are coded T9
VAT Amount	**0.00**	

3 When you are satisfied that your entry is correct CLICK the **Save** button to save the details to disk. The information that you have entered is simply recorded for use at a later time when the details are posted to the ledgers during the month end procedures.

4 PRESS [Esc] to return you to the **Financial Controller** window.

Activity 13.2 Setting up additional recurring entries

In addition to the van loan interest you will have electricity and telephone to pay for. Under prearranged terms you have agreed to pay £80 per month for your electricity and £75 per month for your telephone. Both of these are rated at the standard rate of VAT. Use **Nominal Ledger** codes **7200** for **Electricity** and **7502** for the **Telephone** and set up two additional recurring entries for these transactions.

Task 14 Setting up asset depreciation

➤ **This Task demonstrates how to cater for asset depreciation.**

Erin Fish Supplies is now the proud possessor of a refrigeration unit and a van. These two items are assets and like all assets of this nature they lose value as time progresses. This loss of value - or depreciation - can be accounted for within the Sage Sterling Accounting system by using the **Depreciation** facility offered within the **Nominal Ledger.**

ENSURE that the **Nominal Ledger** window is on display.

Activity 14.1 To set up asset depreciation

1 From the **Nominal Ledger** window CLICK the **Features** menu command.

2 CLICK the **Depreciation** option and enter the following:

N/C	**0021**	(Plant/Machinery Depreciation - use the **Finder**)
Description	**Refrigeration unit**	
Value	**3600.00**	
Tp	**R**	Reducing balance
%	**15.00**	15% reduction in value from previous year's value

3 CLICK the **N/C** column in the box beneath **0021** and the following will appear:

Amount	48.43	The amount of next month's depreciation. This is calculated automatically by the system
Current	3600.00	Automatically entered by the system

4 When you are satisfied that the details are correct CLICK the **Save** button to save the details to disk. The information that you have entered is simply recorded for use at a later time when the details are posted to the ledgers during the month end procedures.

Activity 14.2 To post a further asset depreciation

The van, currently valued at £8000, is liable to an annual straight line depreciation (coded by the letter S) of 25%. Use the Nominal Code **0051** for **Motor Vehicles Depreciation** and save this asset's depreciation to the disk file.

When your entries are complete and saved, PRESS [Esc] to return to the **Financial Controller** window.

Section B

Starting the first month's trading

Task 15 Setting up further supplier details

➤ **The purpose of this Task is to reinforce and test the ability to set up supplier details and to learn how to post opening balances.**

Before Erin Fish Supplies can begin making a profit it must have some stock to sell. The company already has a number of suppliers with whom it has been dealing in the past. Accounts containing the names and addresses of these suppliers need to be created in the **Purchase Ledger**. In addition, because the company still owes some of them money from purchases made prior to 1st August 19XX we must also record their opening balances.

Ensure that the **Financial Controller** window is being displayed and from this window CLICK the **Suppliers** button.

Activity 15.1 Entering further supplier details

You have already seen how to enter supplier details in Task 6. To give you more practice in performing this operation CLICK the **Record** button on the **Suppliers** window.

1 ENTER the following supplier's details into the **Supplier Record** window:

A/C **WILL**

Name	**P Williams**
Street 1	**4 Front View**
Street 2	
Town	**Seaporth**
County	
Post Code	**SE2 1LI**
Contact	**Phil**
Telephone	**0345 678912**
Fax	
Analysis 1	**S1**
Analysis 2	
Analysis 3	
Department	(Leave at the default 1)
Tax ID	**234567891**

2 Change the **Defaults** to:

Nominal	**1001**
Tax Code	**T0**

3 When you are satisfied that you have correctly entered all this information CLICK the **Save** button to post the details to the **Purchase Ledger** and to clear the information from the **Supplier Record** window.

4 CONTINUE by entering all the following details:

A/C	**HISEA**
Name	**MV Hisea**
Street 1	**Berth 2**
Street 2	**Canary Dock**
Town	**Upton-on-Sea**
County	
Post Code	**UP1 2WQ**
Contact	**Rod**
Telephone	**0456 789123**
Fax	
Analysis 1	**S2**
Analysis 2	
Analysis 3	
Department	(Leave at the default 1)
Tax ID	**345678912**

5 CHANGE the **Terms** to:

Credit Limit	**2000**

6 CONTINUE by entering in the **Defaults** box:

Nominal	1001
Tax Code	T0

7 CLICK the **Save** button to post the information to the **Purchase Ledger.**

8 ENTER the details of the next three suppliers:

A/C	**ABC**
Name	**ABC Fishery**
Street 1	**Shark House**
Street 2	**Myrtle Street**
Town	**Atlantica**
County	
Post Code	**AL3 6VH**
Contact	**Jack**
Telephone	**0567 891234**
Fax	
Analysis 1	**S3**
Analysis 2	
Analysis 3	
Department	**(Leave at the default 1)**
Tax ID	**456789123**
Credit Limit	**3000**
Nominal	**1001**
Tax Code	**T0**

A/C	**SMILE**
Name	**H Smiley**
Street 1	**Seacroft**
Street 2	**Shell Terrace**
Town	**Sewed**
County	
Post Code	**SE4 9OP**
Contact	**Theo**
Telephone	**0678 912345**
Fax	
Analysis 1	**S4**
Analysis 2	
Analysis 3	
Department	**(Leave at the default 1)**
Tax ID	**567891234**
Nominal	**1001**
Tax Code	**T0**

A/C	**WOOD**
Name	**T Feller**
Street 1	**Dark Wood**
Street 2	**Glade Green**
Town	**Timberland**
County	
Post Code	**T1 1T**
Contact	**Pan**
Telephone	**0789 123456**
Fax	
Analysis 1	**S5**
Analysis 2	
Analysis 3	
Department	(Leave at the default 1)
Tax ID	**67891234**
Credit Limit	**1000**
Nominal	**1001**
Tax Code	**T1** (Leave as the default value)

Notice the amounts listed under **Credit Limit**. This refers to the credit the supplier has given to your company. These accounts are monthly accounts and must be settled by the fifteenth day of the month following delivery. For those suppliers giving no credit the terms are cash on delivery. By cash it will be understood that a cheque will suffice. We shall deal with the handling of cash later in the Training Guide.

Each supplier also has an Analysis Code listed. These range from S1 to S5 and we shall see the use that these can be put to later.

When you have posted the details of the last supplier PRESS Esc to return to the **Suppliers** window where you will see all six suppliers listed in the information panel.

Activity 15.2 Posting opening balances

Your suppliers' opening balances could have been posted during the supplier record set-up. However, when this is done no account is taken of VAT in the opening balance - any tax amount is contained within the gross amount. To retain any tax details the opening balances will be entered by following the same procedure used to enter purchase invoices which you have already done in Task 7. The only difference is in the references used. From the **Suppliers** window CLICK the **Invoice** button to reveal the **Supplier Invoice** form.

1 ENTER the following opening balance:

A/C	**HISEA**	Use the **Finder** and the name of the account holder is automatically entered along with the default date
Date	**01/08/XX**	Change the default date

Ref	**O/Bal**	
N/C	**9998**	Use the **Finder**
Description	**Opening Balance**	
Amount	**854.79**	
T/c	**T0**	

2 CLICK the **Department** button to reveal the **Transaction Posting** window and you will see the default Department is 1. This is the department all the suppliers have been assigned to and we shall say more about departments later in the Guide.

3 CLICK the **Ok** button to return to the **Supplier Invoice** form.

4 CLICK the **Save** button to post the invoice details to the ledgers and to clear the information that you have just entered from the screen.

5 REPEAT this procedure by entering the following opening balance:

A/C	**WOOD**	Use the **Finder** and the name of the account holder is automatically entered
Date	**01/08/XX**	Change the default date
Ref	**O/Bal**	
N/C	**9998**	Use the **Finder**
Description	**Opening Balance**	
Amount	**132.64**	
T/c	**T1**	
VAT Amount	**23.21**	This is automatically calculated

The **Nominal Ledger** code 9998 is called the **Suspense Account** and is used only for opening balances. Notice also the Invoice reference of O/Bal which is used for opening balances.

When you have completed the posting of these two opening balances PRESS Esc to close the window and return to the **Suppliers** window where you will see the two opening balances displayed.

Accounting performed:

The Creditors Control Account is *credited* with the gross amount.
The Nominal Suspense Account is *debited* with the net amount.
The Purchase Tax Control Account is *debited* with the VAT.

Task 16

Entering and paying further purchase invoices

➤ **The purpose of this Task is to reinforce and test the ability to post purchase invoices and their payments.**

Having opened the supplier accounts we must now post the company's purchases to their respective accounts and, for those suppliers that do not give the company credit, we must also post the payments for the purchases. Both of these procedures you have already performed in Tasks 7 and 8.

Whenever purchase invoices are to be posted it is good practice to check the figures on the invoice to see that no error has been made. You can use the **Calculator** that is accessible via the **Utilities menu** command to do this.

Activity 16.1 Posting further purchase invoices

1 From the **Suppliers** window CLICK the **Invoice** button and post the following purchase invoices using the **Nominal Account** name **Stock** with code **1001** and Department **1:**

Purchase Invoice No. 124 (this is entered under **Ref**)

T Feller
Dark Wood
Glade Green
Timberland T1 1T

Date: 5 Aug XX

Supply to Erin Fish Supplies

25 Tonnes cut timber @ £15.00 per tonne

		£
Value	:	375.00
VAT	:	65.63
Total	:	440.63

Terms: Monthly Account

Purchase Invoice No. 003042

MV Hisea
Berth 2
Canary Dock
Upton-on-Sea UP1 2WQ

Date: 4 Aug XX

Supply to Erin Fish Supplies

250 dozen scallops @ £6.00 per dozen

	£
Value	1500.00
VAT	0.00
Total	1500.00

Terms Monthly Account

Purchase Invoice No. 2771

P Williams
4 Front View
Seaporth SE2 1LI

Date: 9 Aug XX

Supply to Erin Fish Supplies

10,000 oysters @ £0.25 each

	£
Value	2500.00
VAT	0.00
Total	2500.00

Terms: COD

Note the abbreviation COD for Cash On Delivery.

3 When the three invoices have been satisfactorily entered PRESS Esc twice in succession to return to the **Financial Controller** window.

Activity 16.2 Posting payments for further purchase invoices

Because the invoice from P Williams was issued under the terms of cash on delivery this order was paid for when it was delivered. This payment will now have to be posted to the **Purchase Ledger**. You have already followed this procedure in Task 8.

1 CLICK the **Bank** button to reveal the **Bank Accounts** window.

2 CLICK the **Supplier** button to reveal the **Supplier Cheque** window.

3 ENTER the details of the payment to the WILL account:

£2500 in respect of P Williams' invoice number 2771 - the cheque number that you used is 3.

4 When the details are correctly entered CLICK the box beneath the heading **Paid.**

5 CLICK the **Pay in Full** button.

6 CLICK the **Remittance** button to reveal the **Remittance Advice** window.

7 CLICK the **Printer** radio button in the **Output** box and then CLICK the **Ok** button to produce a remittance advice slip to accompany your payment.

8 CLICK the **Save** button.

9 PRESS Esc twice in succession to return to the **Financial Controller** window.

Task 17 Setting up the stock details

➤ **In this Task you will learn how to set up the stock details for each individual stock item.**

All purchases are sold on from stock. The company has a refrigeration unit to store fish stock and a yard to store the timber. However, there will be many times when the company will make a sale without actually having had a delivery. For example, you may find a customer for timber on the mainland so it would be counter productive to have the timber delivered to the island only to send it back to the mainland again. As a consequence the timber would not have been physically stored as stock. However, despite this fact, proper accounting procedure requires that you enter the timber as stock so that the purchase transaction shows it being put into accounted stock and the subsequent sale transaction shows it as being accounted for out of stock.

There are two stages in recording the purchases of new stock items:

- All the details relating to the description of the stock are recorded with the exception of the quantity to be put into stock.
- The quantity of stock is then recorded as having been put into stock.

We have three purchases to enter into stock.

Activity 18.1 Posting the timber details to stock

1 From the **Financial Controller** window CLICK the **Products** button to reveal the **Products** window:

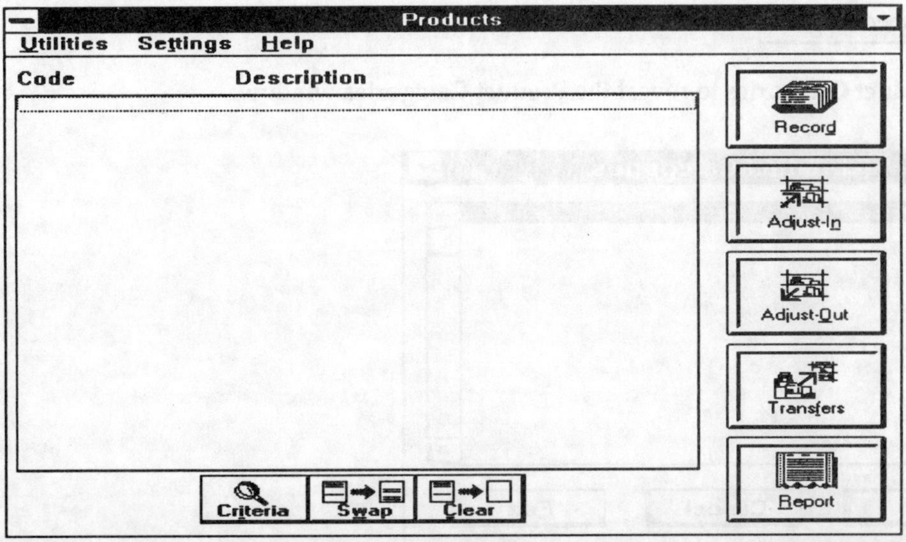

Notice that the information panel is empty as we have not yet entered any stock details.

2 CLICK the **Record** button to reveal the **Product Record** window.

3 ENTER the following information into the **Product Details** box in the **Product Record** window:

Code	**CT**	This refers to Cut Timber
Description	**Cut Timber**	
Tax Code	**T1**	Leave at the default
Sales Price	**30.00**	
Unit of Sale	**Tonne**	
Location	**Yard**	

4 ENTER the following into the **Defaults** box:

Nominal	**1001**

The next box, **Category**, has the default number **1**. We need to define stock categories.

5 CLICK the **Settings** menu on the **Menu bar** to reveal a drop-down menu:

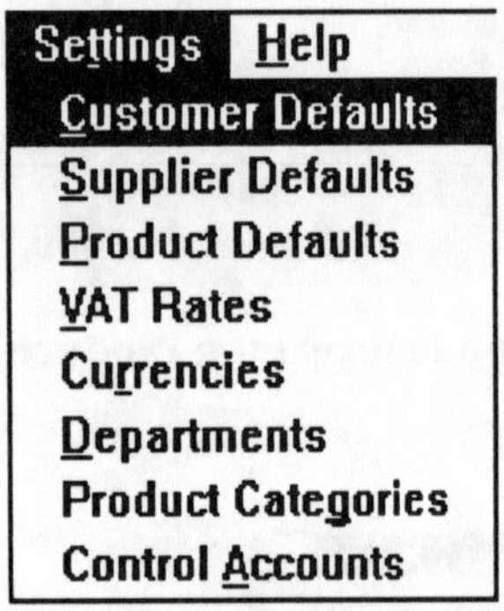

6 CLICK **Product Categories** to reveal the **Product Categories** window:

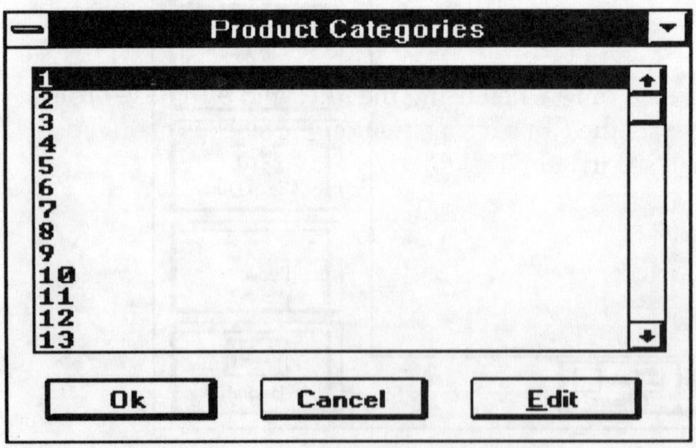

7 CLICK the **Edit** button and ENTER the **Name** as **Timber.**

8 CLICK the **Ok** button and you will see **Category 1 Timber** listed in the **Product Categories** window.

9 CLICK the **Ok** button to return to the **Product Record** window.

Notice that Category 1 has not yet been annotated as Timber. This product record will have to be saved to disk first and then retrieved before the new category annotation can appear.

10 CHANGE **Department** from the default **1** to **3.**

11 ENTER the following into the **Supplier Information** box:

A/C Reference	**WOOD**	Use the **Finder**
Part reference		Leave blank
Re-order level	**5**	

The stock level details in the **Stock Levels** box cannot be entered just yet.

12 CLICK the **Save** button to save this information to disk.

13 CLICK the **Done** button to return to the **Products** window where you will see the code **CT** and **Description Cut Timber** displayed in the information panel.

You will notice that you have not entered the quantity delivered into stock. Indeed, it is not possible to do so at this stage. Just as the **Nominal Ledger** has to balance so the stock control system has to reflect true inputs and true outputs with no possibilities of error. This means that the only way you can change stock quantities in the stock control system is via one of the following procedures:

Adjust-In	to increase the stock level
Adjust-Out	to decrease the stock level
Despatch Sales order	to decrease the stock level
Receive Purchase order	to increase the stock level
Invoicing from stock	to decrease the stock level

The latter three methods can be performed only when using the sales and purchase order processing or the invoicing from stock facilities. In such a situation the stock is changed automatically by the system as we shall see in later Tasks.

Task 18 Entering purchases into stock

➤ **This Task will show you how to post purchases into stock.**

An increase in stock can be entered into the sytem via the **Adjust-In** button on the **Products** window and a decrease can be entered by the **Adjust-Out** button.

Activity 18.1 Posting the purchased timber quantity to stock

From the **Products** window CLICK the **Adjust-In** button to reveal the **Stock** window in which is displayed an **Adjustments In** form:

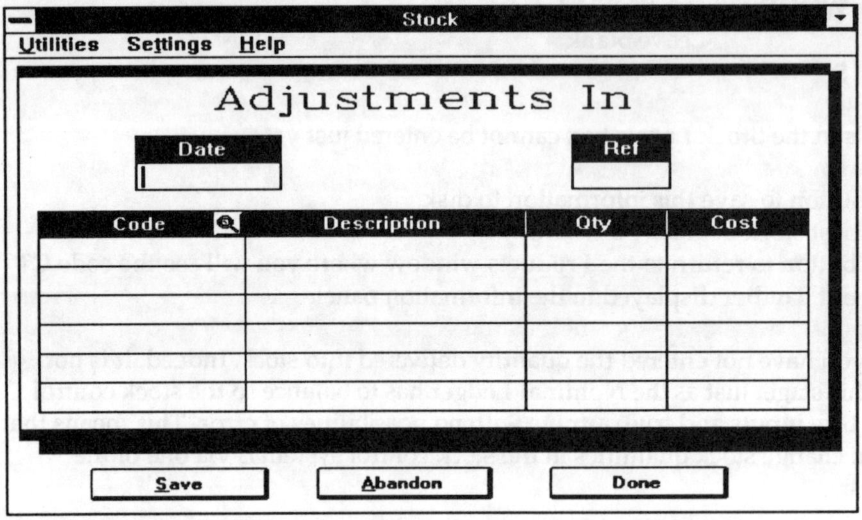

1 ENTER the following information into this screen:

Date	**05/08/XX**	
Ref	**WOOD**	
Code	**CT**	Use the **Finder**
Description	**Timber delivery**	
Qty	**25**	
Cost	**15**	This is the unit cost that you enter here

2 When you are satisfied that all the details are correct CLICK the **Save** button.

3 PRESS Esc to close the **Adjustments In** window and return to the **Products** window.

Activity 18.2 **Checking the stock details**

In the information panel of the **Products** window you will see the recently entered stock with **Code CT** and **Description Cut Timber** displayed.

1 CLICK the description to highlight it in *reverse video.*

2 CLICK the **Record** button and the screen then fills with the details of the stock item that you have just entered. Notice the **In Stock** and **Cost Price** entries have been updated as a consequence of the previous Activity. Notice also that **Category 1** is now annotated as **Timber.**

3 PRESS [Esc] to close the window and return to the **Products** window.

Activity 18.3 **Posting further stock details**

Having seen how to post stock details you will now be able to post the two further stock details yourself.

1 CLICK the **Clear** button to clear the current selection in the **Products** window.

2 CLICK the **Record** button.

3 ENTER the following information into the **Product Details** box in the **Product Record** window:

Code	**FS**	This refers to Scallops
Description	**Scallops**	
Tax Code	**T0**	
Sales Price	**9.00**	
Unit of Sale	**Dozen**	
Location	**Fridge**	

4 ENTER the following into the **Defaults** box:

Nominal	**1001**
Category	**2**

5 CLICK **Settings** in the **Menu bar** to display the drop-down menu and then CLICK **Product Categories.**

6 In the **Product Categories** window CLICK the number **2** and then CLICK the **Edit** button.

7 ENTER **Scallops** as the name of Category 2.

8 CHANGE **Department** from the default **1** to **3**.

9 ENTER the following into the **Supplier Information** box:

A/C Reference	**HISEA**	
Part reference		Leave blank
Re-order level	**50**	

10 CLICK the **Save** button to save the information to disk.

11 ENTER the following information into the **Product Details** box in the **Product Record** window:

Code	**FO**	This refers to Oysters
Description	**Oysters**	
Tax Code	**T0**	
Sales Price	**0.35**	
Unit of Sale	**Each**	
Location	**Fridge**	

12 ENTER the following into the **Defaults** box:

Nominal	**1001**
Category	**3**

13 DEFINE the Name of Category 3 as **Oysters**.

14 CHANGE the default Department from **1** to **3**.

15 ENTER the following into the **Supplier Information** box:

A/C Reference	**WILL**	
Part reference		Leave blank
Re-order level	**1000**	

16 CLICK the **Save** button to save the information to disk.

17 PRESS [Esc] to return to the **Products** window where you will see all three items of stock listed in the information panel.

18 CLICK all three stock descriptions in the information panel of the **Products** window to highlight them.

19 CLICK the **Record** button to review the state of your stock. CLICK the **Next** and **Prev** buttons in the **Product Record** window to range through the stock items.

20 When you are satisfied that everything has been entered correctly PRESS [Esc] twice in succession to return to the **Financial Controller** window.

Activity 18.4 Posting the fish purchases to stock

Having seen how to post purchases to stock you will now be able to use the **Adjust-In** button in the **Products** window to place your purchases into stock. Refer to Task 16 for the details of the purchase invoices.

When you have done this CHECK your postings via the **Record** button in the **Products** window.

Task 19 Setting up customer details

➤ **In this Task you will learn how to post a customer's name, address and account details.**

Having purchased stock the company is now in a position to start selling. All sales are recorded through the **Sales Ledger** which is accessible via the **Customers** button in the **Financial Controller** window. As with the **Purchase Ledger**, before sale transactions can be posted to the ledgers the customer details must be recorded in the **Sales Ledger**. This procedure is entirely similar to the one used for supplier details.

Activity 19.1 Posting Customer Details into the Sales Ledger

1 From the **Financial Controller** window CLICK the **Customers** button to reveal the **Customers** window.

2 CLICK the **Record** button to reveal the **Customer Record** window.

3 ENTER the following information into this screen:

A/C	**JONES**	
Name	**A Jones**	
Street 1	**Fish Merchant**	
Street 2	**38 Sole Walk**	
Town	**Codton**	
County		
Post Code	**CO1 2DD**	
Contact	**Alan**	
Telephone	**0891 234567**	
Fax		
Analysis 1	**C1**	
Analysis 2		
Analysis 3		
Department	**2**	(Change from the default 1)
Tax ID	**789123456**	
Credit Limit	**2000**	
Nominal	**1001**	
Tax Code	**T0**	

4 When you are satisfied that all the details are correct then CLICK the **Save** button to post the details to the **Sales Ledger** and clear the **Customer Record** window.

Activity 19.2 Posting further customer details to the Sales Ledger

To give you some practice at posting customer details post the following to the **Sales Ledger**:

A/C	**SMITH**
Name	**F Smith & Son**
Street 1	**Ace Fishery**
Street 2	**Stall 6**
Town	**Haddie Market**
County	**Haddie**
Post Code	**HA3 4RT**
Contact	**Fred**
Telephone	**0912 345678**
Fax	
Analysis 1	**C2**
Analysis 2	
Analysis 3	
Department	**2**
Tax ID	**891234567**
Credit Limit	**2000.00**
Nominal	**1001**
Tax Code	**T0**

A/C	**LEE**
Name	**Lee Ling**
Street 1	**House of Peking**
Street 2	**177 Canton Row**
Town	**Seatonne**
County	
Post Code	**SE6 6TH**
Contact	**Lee**
Telephone	**0834 126578**
Fax	**0834 126875**
Analysis 1	**C3**
Analysis 2	
Analysis 3	
Department	**2**
Tax ID	**912345678**
Credit Limit	**1000.00**
Nominal	**1001**
Tax Code	**T0**

A/C	**BLUE**
Name	**Blue Yonder Restaurants**
Street 1	**14 Alley Walk**
Street 2	
Town	**Norsea**
County	
Post Code	**NO1 8EF**
Contact	**Bill**
Telephone	**0447 391634**
Fax	**0447 391635**
Analysis 1	**C4**
Analysis 2	
Analysis 3	
Department	**2**
Tax ID	**192837465**
Nominal	**1001**
Tax Code	**T0**

A/C	**OACH**
Name	**R Oach & P Ike**
Street 1	**Fish Merchants**
Street 2	**Humerton Wharf**
Town	**Humerton**
County	
Post Code	**HU6 6YG**
Contact	**Bob**
Telephone	**0332 875335**
Fax	
Analysis 1	**C5**
Analysis 2	
Analysis 3	
Department	**2**
Tax ID	**928374651**
Nominal	**1001**
Tax Code	**T0**

A/C	**CASUAL**
Name	**Casual Sales**
Street 1	**Casual**
Street 2	
Town	

County
Post Code
Contact
Telephone
Fax

Analysis 1 **C6**
Analysis 2
Analysis 3
Department **2**
Tax ID

Nominal **1001**
Tax Code **T1**

Notice the amounts listed under **Credit Limit**. This refers to the credit your company has granted to the customer. These accounts are monthly accounts and must be settled by the fifteenth day of the month following delivery. For those customers to whom no credit has been given the terms are cash on delivery. By cash it will be understood that a cheque will suffice. We shall deal with the handling of cash later in the Guide.

When you have saved the CASUAL details to disk PRESS [Esc] to close the **Customers Record** window and to return to the **Customers** window where you will see the six customers listed in the information panel.

Activity 19.3 Posting opening balances

Posting opening balances follows the same procedure used to enter purchase invoices which you have already done in Task 15. The only difference is in the references used. From the **Customers** window CLICK the **Invoice** button to reveal the display of a **Customer Invoice** form.

1 ENTER the following opening balances:

A/C	**JONES**	Use the **Finder** and the account holder's name is entered automatically along with the default date which will have to be amended
Date	**01/08/XX**	
Ref	**O/Bal**	
N/C	**9998**	Use the **Finder**
Description	**Opening Balance**	
Amount	**1326.04**	
T/c	**T0**	

2 CLICK the **Save** button to save these details to disk.

3 When the form clears, ENTER the following into the blank form:

A/C	**OACH**	Use the **Finder** and the account holder's name is entered automatically
Date	**01/08/XX**	
Ref	**O/Bal**	
N/C	**9998**	Use the **Finder**
Description	**Opening Balance**	
Amount	**2648.14**	
T/c	**T0**	

4 CLICK the **Save** button to save these details to disk.

The **Nominal Ledger** code 9998 is called the **Suspense Account** and is used only for opening balances. Notice also the Invoice reference of O/Bal which is used for opening balances.

5 When both opening balances are recorded PRESS [Esc] to return to the **Customers** window where you will see the two balances recorded against the accounts JONES and OACH in the information panel.

6 PRESS [Esc] to return to the **Financial Controller** window.

Task 20 Raising an invoice from stock

➤ **In this Task you will learn how to produce an invoice from stock.**

During the course of the month of August the company has sold timber to a variety of customers. The maximum load sold is usually around one tonne which sells for £30. To avoid raising a large number of accounts for small amounts of money you have decided to sell your timber via the *casual account* and to lump the entire month's sales into one amount. In reality no invoices were issued for these transactions but to follow proper accounting procedures a single invoice will be issued for the full month's sales. This will demonstrate how the invoice production procedure automatically reduces the stock level by the appropriate amount.

The invoicing procedure consists of three parts:

Invoice creation
The invoice is created by entering the customer and sale details, followed by the header details that appear at the top of the order form. Finally, the footer details are entered that appear at the bottom of the order form.

Printing
The invoice is printed for onward transmission to the customer.

Ledger updating
The ledgers are updated with the information on the invoice and the stock is reduced by the appropriate amount.

Activity 20.1 To raise an invoice from stock

1 From the **Financial Controller** window CLICK the **Invoicing** button to display the **Customer Invoice** window.

2 CLICK the **Stock** button to reveal the **Invoice** window.

3 ENTER into the **Invoice** window the following information:

Sold To:	**CASUAL**	Use the **Finder**
Invoice No:	**1**	This number is automatically allocated by the system
Date:	**31/08/XX**	

4 ENTER the following information into the lower portion of the **Invoice** window:

Stock Code	**CT**	Use the **Finder**

The **Product Item Line** window automatically comes into view:

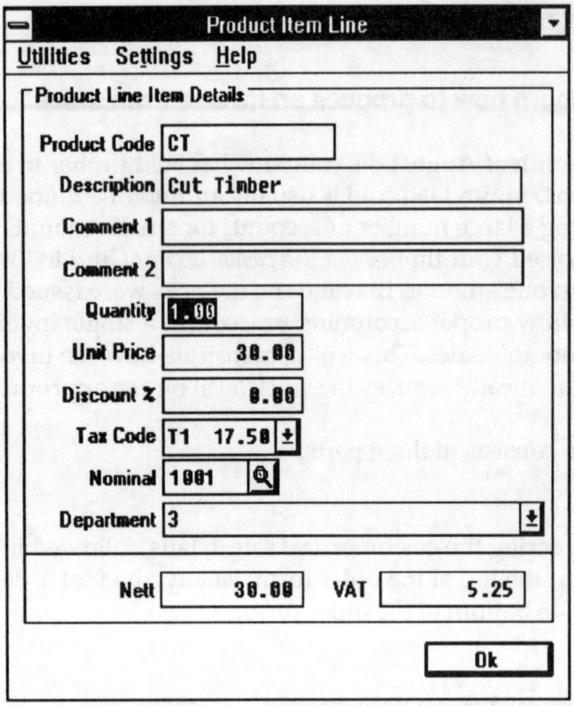

5 ENTER the quantity sold into this window - you will see that the **Quantity** box is highlighted in *reverse video* and is currently displaying the default quantity of 1.00:

Quantity **22**

Entering this amount completes the invoice stock items.

6 CLICK the **Ok** button to close the **Product Item Line** window and return to a completed **Invoice.**

This completes the details for the body of the invoice. Next the header details are entered.

7 CLICK the **Order** button to reveal the **Order Details** window.

8 ENTER the following details into the **Order Details** window (when the invoice is printed these will appear at its head):

Order No. **1**
Deliver To. **Casual**
Notes 1 **August's casual timber sales**

9 CLICK the **Ok** button to close this window and return to the **Invoice** window.

10 CLICK the **Footer** button to reveal the **Footer Details** window.

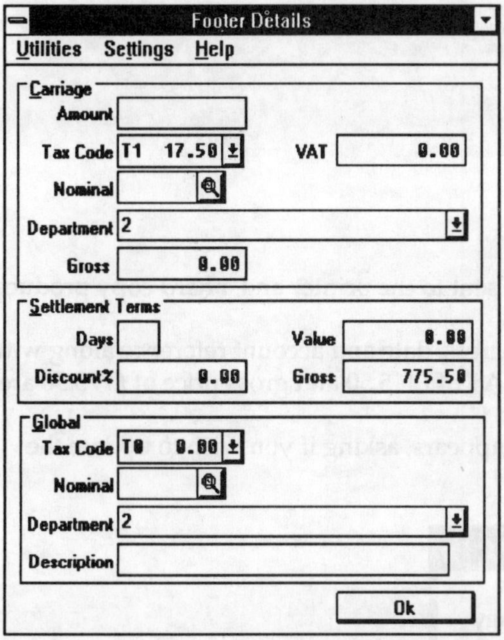

11 CHANGE the **Tax Code** in the **Global** box to **T1**.

12 ENTER the **Nominal** in the **Global** box as **1001**.

13 CLICK the **Ok** button to close this window and return to the **Invoice** window.

14 CLICK the **Batch** button to store the details of the invoice on disk.

We could have printed directly from the **Invoice** window but instead we have chosen to save the invoice to disk first to demonstrate that invoices can be printed in batches as well as separately.

15 CLICK the **Done** button to close the invoice window and return to the **Customer Invoice** window where you will see the outstanding invoice displayed in the information panel.

You have now completed all the details necessary for the generation of an invoice.

Activity 20.2 To produce a hard copy of the invoice

1 From the **Customer Invoice** window CLICK the **Print Batch** button to reveal the **Invoice Printing** window advising you to check that your printer is in order:

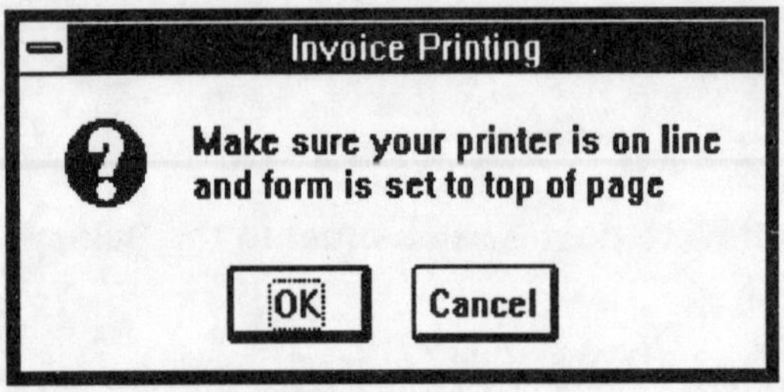

2 CLICK the **Ok** button and the invoice will be sent to the printer and a hard copy produced.

The invoice contains the company name and address, date and account reference along with the details of the sale. The net price of £660.00, VAT of £115.50 and gross price of £775.50 are also shown.

During the printing the **Batch Print** window appears, asking if you wish to update the ledgers with any outstanding entries.

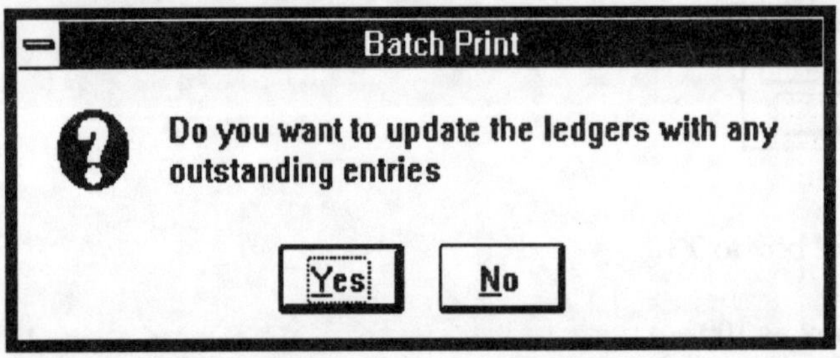

We do have outstanding entries and we could click the **Yes** button here and have the ledgers and stock updated with the details from this invoice. Instead we shall update the ledgers in a separate Activity.

3 CLICK the **No** button.

Notice the tick under the word **Print** in the top right-hand corner of the information panel of the **Product** window that indicates that a hard copy of this invoice has been produced.

4 When the invoice has been printed PRESS Esc to return to the **Financial Controller** window.

Task 21 Entry of a sales invoice and viewing the stock

➤ **In this Task you will learn how to post a sales order to the Sales Ledger.**

Having produced an invoice from stock it is now time to post the details of the sale to the ledgers.

Activity 21.1 Posting a sale

1 From the **Financial Controller** window CLICK the **Invoicing** button.

2 CLICK the **Update** button to reveal the **Update Ledgers** window:

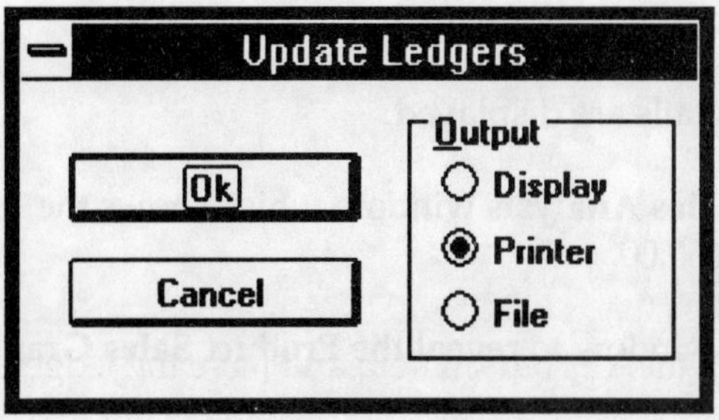

3 CLICK the **Display** radio button in the **Output** box.

4 CLICK the **Ok** button

A report is sent to the monitor screen displayed in a window called **File View**. The report describes the details of the CASUAL invoice. Use the slider bar at the bottom of the window to scroll the report sideways.

5 DOUBLE CLICK the **Control-menu** box to return to the **Customer Invoice** window and there under the word **Post** in the information panel you will see a second tick to indicate that this particular invoice has been posted to the ledgers.

6 PRESS Esc to return to the **Financial Controller** window

Accounting performed:

The Debtors Control Account is *credited* with the gross amount.
The Stock Nominal Account 1001 is *debited* with the net amount.
The VAT Control Account is *debited* with the tax.

Activity 21.2 Viewing the stock

1 From the **Financial Controller** window CLICK the **Products** button to reveal the **Products** window with all three items of stock listed in the information panel.

2 CLICK the **Swap** button below the information panel of the **Products** window to highlight all the stock items in *reverse video*.

3 CLICK the **Record** button to reveal the **Stock Record** window displaying the details of the first item of stock - timber.

The details of the company's timber stock will now be seen to consist of just 3 tonnes. This is below the re-order level so the re-order quantity must be ordered from T Feller in readiness for next month's sales.

4 CLICK the **Next** button at the bottom of the **Product Record** window to view the next item of stock - the oysters.
CLICK the **Next** button again to view the state of the scallops stock.

5 CLICK the **Prev** button until the timber stock details are displayed.

6 CLICK the **Sales** button to reveal the **Product Sales Analysis** window which shows the **Quantity Sold** to be 22 and the **Sales Value** as 660.00.

7 CLICK the **Graphs** button in the bottom of this window to reveal the **Product Sales Graph** window.

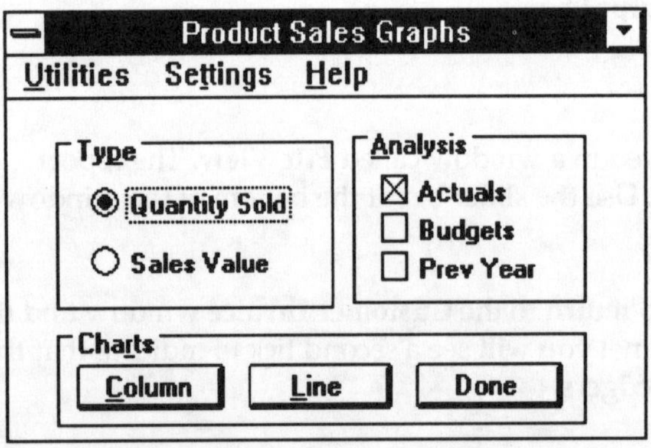

8 CLICK the **Sales Value** radio button in the **Type** box and ENSURE that a cross is located in the square beside **Actuals** in the **Analysis** box.

9 CLICK the **Column** button in the **Charts** box to reveal a graphical display of your sales - a single bar in a bar chart.

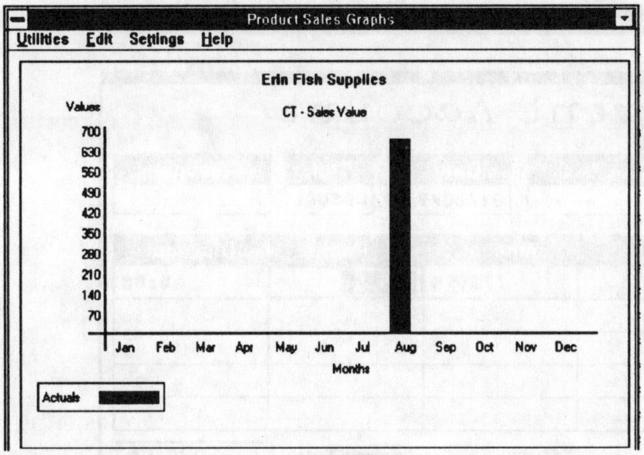

10 CLICK the **Line** box in this window to change the display to a line graph. This line graph is telling you that since your sale of timber your revenue has fallen to zero.

11 PRESS [Esc] five times in succession to return to the **Financial Controller** window.

Activity 21.4 Posting a bank receipt for a sale

All the timber sales were cash on delivery so during the course of the month you would have been paying money received for timber into the bank. These must now be recorded as a single bank receipt and posted to the ledger.

1 From the **Financial Controller** window CLICK the **Bank** button to reveal the **Bank Accounts** window.

2 CLICK the **Customer** button to reveal the **Customer Receipts** window containing a **Bank Current Account** form.

3 ENTER the bank receipt of £775.50 using the following details:

A/C	**CASUAL**	Use the **Finder**
Date	**31/08/XX**	
Ref	**CASUAL**	

Notice that as soon as you enter the account name CASUAL all outstanding invoices are displayed. In this case there is only one invoice.

Notice also that the **Pay in Full** button cannot be activated yet.

4 CLICK the **Paid** box to the immediate right of the 775.00 to activate the **Paid in Full** button.

5 CLICK the **Pay in Full** button and 775.50 is automatically entered into the **Paid** column:

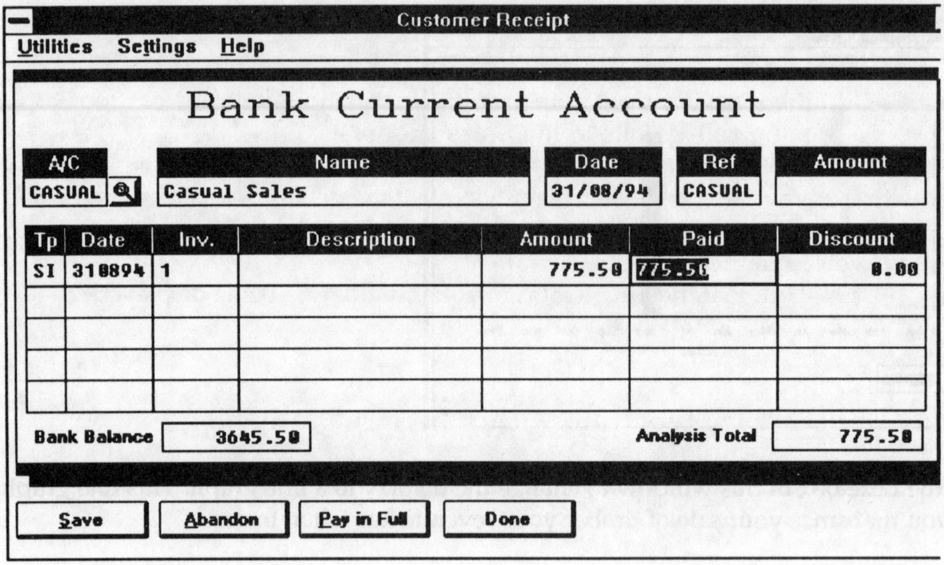

6 CLICK the **Save** button.

7 CLICK the **Done** button.

8 PRESS Esc to return to the **Financial Controller** window.

Activity 21.5 Checking the posting

1 From the **Financial Controller** window CLICK the **Nominal** button.

2 CLICK the account **1200 Bank Current Account** to highlight it in *reverse video*.

3 CLICK the **Activity** button to reveal the **Nominal Ledger Transaction History** window in which is displayed the transaction history of the bank account and in particular the posting of 775.50.

4 PRESS Esc twice in succession to return to the **Financial Controller** window.

Task 22 Raising further invoices

➤ **In this Task you will gain practice in raising invoices from stock and posting sale details to the Sales Ledger.**

In the previous Task it was mentioned that the details of a sale can be posted to all the appropriate ledgers using the **Update Ledgers** facility available within the **Invoice Production** facility.

ENSURE that the **Financial Controller** window is being displayed.

Activity 22.1 Updating ledgers from within Invoice Production

1 The following is a sale. From the **Financial Controller** window CLICK the **Invoicing button** and in the **Customer Invoice** window CLICK the **Stock** button.

2 ENTER the following invoice into the system via **Invoicing from Stock.**

Sold To:	**JONES**	Use the **Finder**
Invoice No:	**2**	**This number is automatically allocated by the system**
Date:	**06/08/XX**	

3 ENTER the following information into the lower portion of the **Invoice** window:

Stock Code **FS**

4 Enter the following details into the **Product Item Line** window:

Quantity **80**

5 CLICK the **Ok** button to return to the **Customer Invoice** window.

6 CLICK the **Order** button and ENTER the following:

Order No. **2**
Deliver To **A Jones**
Address1 **As per invoice**

7 CLICK the **Ok** button to return to the **Customer Invoice** window.

8 CLICK the **Footer** button and AMEND the **Footer** details in the **Global** box as:

Nominal **1001**

9 CLICK the **Ok** button when you are satisfied that all is correct.

10 CLICK the **Print** button and send the invoice to the printer for a hard copy.

During the printing of the invoice the **Invoice Printing** window comes into view

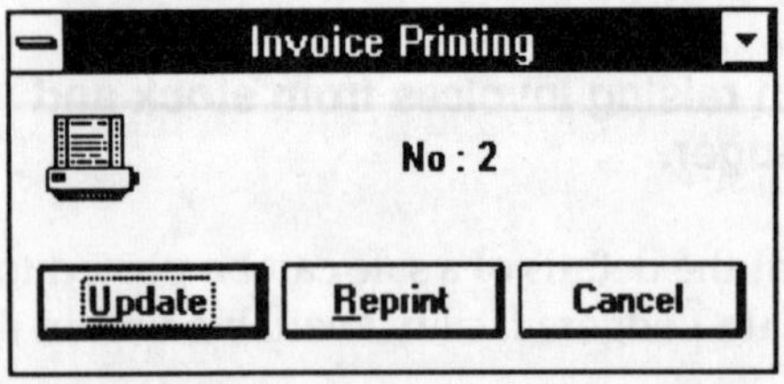

11 When the invoice has been printed CLICK the **Update** button in the **Invoice Printing** window.

This causes the **Update Ledger** window to appear.

12 CLICK the **Display** radio button in the **Output** box and then CLICK the **Ok** button to update the ledgers.

A **File View** window appears displaying the details of the transaction.

13 DOUBLE CLICK the **Control-menu** box to close the **File View** window and return to a blank **Invoice** form.

14 PRESS Esc to return to the **Customer Invoice** window where you will see from the ticks beneath **Print/Post** in the information panel that the invoice has been both printed and posted.

15 PRESS Esc to return you to the **Financial Controller** window.

Activity 22.2 Checking the Sales Invoices display

1 From the **Financial Controller** window CLICK the **Customers** button.

2 From the **Customers** window CLICK the JONES account description to highlight it in *reverse video.*

3 CLICK the **Activity** button to reveal the **Aged Debtors Analysis** window where you will see that his balance exceeds his credit limit.

4 CLICK the **History** button to reveal the **Customer Transaction History** window that is displaying the transaction history of the JONES account, namely the opening balance and this last sale. The asterisk at the side of a value indicates an unpaid transaction. Notice that A Jones' balance exceeds his credit limit.

5 PRESS Esc three times in succession to return to the **Financial Controller** window.

Activity 22.3 Checking the Nominal Ledger display

1 From the **Financial Controller** window CLICK the **Nominal** button and in the **Nominal Ledger** window information panel CLICK the account **1001 Stock** to highlight it in *reverse video.*

2 CLICK the **Activity** button to reveal the **Nominal Ledger Transaction History** window in which you will see the transaction history of the Nominal Account code 1001 called Stock. The last transaction entered is the sale to JONES.

3 PRESS [Esc] twice in succession to return to the **Financial Controller** window.

Activity 22.4 Checking the stock details display

1 From the **Financial Controller** window CLICK the **Products** button to reveal the **Stock** window.

2 From the Products window CLICK the **Swap** button to highlight all three stock items in the information panel.

3 CLICK the **Record** button to reveal the **Product Record** window displaying the stock details of the first item of stock. Use the **Next** and **Prev** buttons to review the entire stock. Notice that your scallops have been decreased by the appropriate amount and that you now have 170 dozen scallops in stock.

4 PRESS [Esc] twice in succession to return to the **Financial Controller** window.

Activity 22.5 Raising further invoices

To familiarise yourself with the manipulations involved in the raising of invoices and the updating of the ledgers:

1 ENTER the following two sales invoices into the system:

Sold To	**OACH**
Invoice No	**3**
Date	**11/08/XX**

2 This sale involves two items. ENTER the first item into the first line of the invoice and the second item into the second line:

Stock Code	**FO**	Use the **Finder**
Quantity	**2000**	

Stock Code **FS** Use the **Finder**
Quantity **50**

3 LEAVE the other items with their default values and ENTER the following into the **Global** box of the **Footer Details** window:

Nominal **1001**

4 In the **Invoice** window CLICK the **Batch** button to save the details to disk and to clear the form.

5 ENTER the second invoice:

Sold To **LEE**
Invoice No **4**
Date **20/08/XX**

Stock Code **FO**
Quantity **5000**

When you have entered the Quantity figure of 5000 you notice that the Gross Value of £1750.00 exceeds the Credit Limit of £1000.00. You decide that this balance is too excessive. You decide to amend the order to 2500 and give the customer a 5% discount in compensation.

6 CLICK the **Abandon** button and ENTER the details again with the new **Quantity** of 2500 and the **Discount** of 5% which is entered into the **Product Item Line** window at the same time as the **Quantity**.

7 ENTER the following into the **Global** box of the **Footer Details** window:

Nominal **1001**

8 CLICK the **Batch** button to save the details to disk.

9 PRESS Esc to return to the **Customer Invoice** window.

10 CLICK the **Print Batch** button and print a copy of all the outstanding invoices.

11 When the **Batch Print** window appears asking if you wish to update the ledgers with any outstanding entries, CLICK the **Yes** button.

The **Update Ledgers** window appears.

12 CLICK the **Printer** radio button in the **Output** box and then CLICK the **Ok** button.

13 When the updating procedure is complete PRESS Esc to return to the **Financial Controller** window.

Activity 22.6 Changing a customer's details

You have agreed to Lee Ling's request to increase his credit limit because of his prompt payment and past payment record.

1 From the **Financial Controller** window CLICK the **Customers** button to reveal the **Customers** window.

2 CLICK the account code **LEE** in the information panel to highlight this account description.

3 CLICK the **Record** button to reveal the **Customer Record** window displaying the details of the **LEE** account.

4 CHANGE the **Credit Limit** from **1000.00** to **2000.00**.

5 CLICK the **Save** button to save the amended details to disk.

6 PRESS [Esc] twice in succession to return to the **Financial Controller** window.

Activity 22.7 Posting a further sale transaction

The sale to LEE was less than his order so he paid promptly and requested his credit limit be increased. His payment of £831.25 is now in the bank. Post this transaction as a sale receipt. Use the **Customer Receipt** form available via the **Customer** button in the **Bank Accounts** window and use the details contained in the invoice report issued in Activity 22.5.

When this Activity is complete return to the **Financial Controller** window.

Task 23 Issuing a statement

Issuing a statement

➤ **In this Task you will learn how to issue a statement following the stock delivery to a customer.**

A statement to a customer shows all outstanding payments due. It may also contain a message to the customer telling them, for example, when you expect to receive payment. It is customary practice to send a statement to all credit customers who have outstanding payments to make.

Activity 23.1 Issuing a statement

1 From the **Financial Controller** window CLICK the **Customers** button to reveal the **Customers** window.

2 CLICK the **Statement** button to reveal the **Customer Statement** window.

3 ENTER the following:

Beginning Date	01/08/XX
Ending Date	31/08/XX

4 CLICK the **Printer** radio button in the **Output** box.

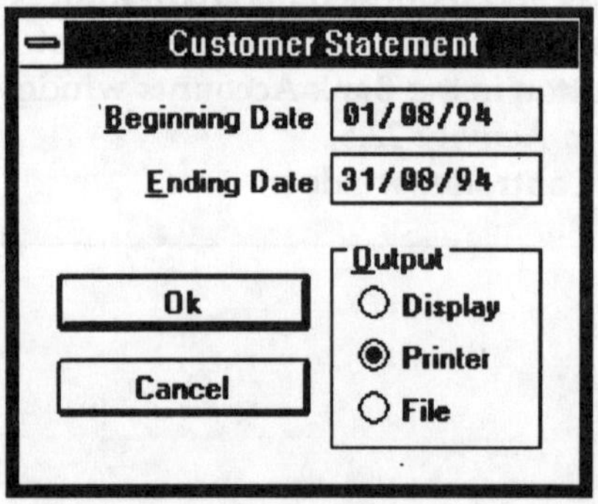

5 CLICK the **Ok** button and your statements will be printed.

6 When the printing is complete PRESS Esc to return to the **Financial Controller** window.

Section C

Order processing

Task 24 Entering a sales order

➤ **In this Task you will learn how to enter orders into the Sales Order Processing facility.**

In Sections A and B you learnt how to enter the details of sales and purchases into the **Sales** and **Purchase Ledgers,** how to raise an invoice from stock based on the details of the sale and how to raise a statement for onward transmission to a customer. Many of these manipulations of the system duplicated earlier ones and in the **Sales** and **Purchase Order Processing** facility such duplicated manipulations are done automatically.

One of the features of the **Sales Order Processing** facility is that it automatically transfers details of a sales order onto an invoice. As a consequence the screen associated with the entry of a sales order is very similar to that used for the production of an invoice from stock. If you refer to Task 20 as you work your way through this Task you will see the similarity.

Activity 24.1 The Sales Order Processing window

1 From the **Financial Controller** window CLICK the **S.O.P** (Sales Order Processing) button to display the **Sales Order Processing** window.

The Sales Order Processing window contains an information panel in which are displayed all the sales orders that are either partially or totally complete within the system. At the moment this panel is empty as there are no such orders yet in existence; we must create the sales orders before they can be displayed here.

Activity 24.2 Filling in the sale details

1 CLICK the **Create** button to reveal the **Create Sales Order** window.

Just as with invoice production there are three parts to the sales order; the Heading, the Stock Items and the Footing. The completion of each part will be a separate activity and the first activity involves entering the items being sold.

2 In the **Create Sales Order** window ENTER the following details into this screen:

To:	**SMITH**	Use the **Finder**
Order No:	**5**	The default is 1 as this is the first time you have used this facility
Date:	**14/08/XX**	
Stock Code	CLICK the **Finder** to reveal the **Product Codes** window	

3 In the **Product Codes** window CLICK the product description with code FO to highlight it and thereby select it.

4 CLICK the **Ok** button in the **Product Codes** window to reveal the **Product Item Line** window.

Here you will see the details of the particular item referred to, namely oysters. Notice that in this window the default amount is 1.

5 AMEND the quantity to be sold from **1** to **3000**.

6 CLICK the **Ok** button to return to the **Create Sales Order** window with all the details pertinent to this item of sale entered upon it.

7 REPEAT this process to add the sale of 50 dozen scallops (code FS) to this order.

This will now complete the sale item details. Next we must fill in the details to be printed on the head of the order.

Activity 24.3 Filling in the order header details

1 From the **Create Sales Order** window with the complete details of the sale on display CLICK the **Order** button to reveal the **Order Details** window.

This window permits you to put in various details that can override the default details associated with the customer. For example, the order may be required to be delivered to an address different from the customer's address and it is here that this would be specified.

2 ENTER the delivery address as:

Deliver To	**F Smith & Son**
Address 1	**As per invoice**

3 When you are satisfied that these details are correct CLICK the **Ok** button to return to the **Create Sales Order** window.

Next we must complete the sales order details by completing the sales order footer.

Activity 24.4 Filling in the order footer details

1 CLICK the **Footer** button in the **Create Sales Order** window to reveal the **Footer Details** window.

There are a number of details that could be entered here relating to carriage and settlement terms. Instead we shall merely consider the box annotated **Global.**

2 In the **Global** box ensure that:

Tax Code	**T0**	
Nominal Code	**1001**	Use the **Finder**
Department	**2**	

3 When you are satisfied that all the details are correct CLICK the **Ok** button to return to the **Create Sales Order** window.

The sales order is now complete insofar as it has been documented within the system. What is now required is for stock to be allocated to the order and for the order to be despatched complete with all documentation. Before we do this we shall set this order to one side and start processing a second sales order.

4 CLICK the **Batch** button to batch the sales order and clear the details of this current sales order from the **Create Sales Order** window.

Activity 24.5 Entering a further sales order

Lee Ling of The House of Peking has just rung through an order for 80 dozen scallops. Using the Account Reference code **LEE** for Lee Ling, **FS** for scallops, Tax Code **T0**, Nominal code **1001** and Department **2,** enter this order into the Sales Order Processing system with the Date **21/08/XX.**

Notice that the order number has been automatically incremented by 1 to 6. When the order has been batched PRESS [Esc] to return to the **Sales Order Processing** window where you will see the two sales orders listed in the information panel.

Task 25 Printing and allocating stock to an order

➤ **In this Task you will learn how stock is allocated to orders within the Sales Order Processing facility.**

When a sales order has first been entered into the system it is rated as a back order. All back orders require to have the appropriate stock allocated to them from the Stock Control facility. Once this has been done the order is rated as an outstanding order - outstanding in the sense that it is still a live order but has not yet been despatched.

Activity 25.1 Allocating stock to an order

1 CLICK the **SMITH** order to highlight it in the information panel.

2 CLICK the **Deliveries** button to reveal the **Sales Order [Enquiries/Deliveries]** window displaying the **SMITH** order with the first item (code FO) highlighted.

3 CLICK the **Complete** button in the **Amend Allocation** box.

The **Amend Allocation** window appears, checking that ALL items are to be allocated with available stock.

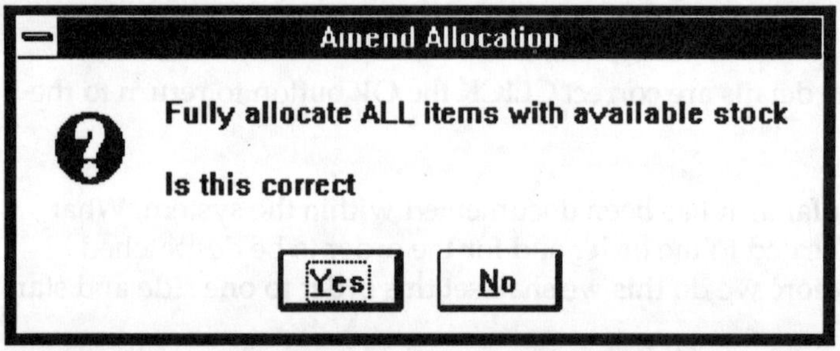

4 CLICK the **Yes** button to return to the **Sales Order [Enquiries/Deliveries]** window where you will see that 3000 oysters and 50 dozen scallops have been allocated on the order.

5 CLICK the **Done** button to return to the **Sales Order Processing** window where you will see the word FULL under **Status** for the SMITH order to indicate that it has been fully allocated from stock.

6 PRESS Esc to return to the **Financial Controller** window and CHECK the stock records via the **Products** button where you will find that 3000 oysters and 50 dozen scallops have been allocated against the current stock levels. This allocated stock will be subtracted from the current stock level only after the goods have been despatched.

7 COMPLETE this Activity with the **Sales Order Processing** window on display.

Activity 25.2 Printing an order

1 From the **Sales Order Processing** window CLICK the description of the SMITH sales order to highlight it and thereby select it.

2 CLICK the **Print Batch** button to reveal the **Sales Order Printing** window.

3 CLICK the **Ok** button and during the printing the **Batch Print** window appears, asking if you wish to allocate any outstanding stock.

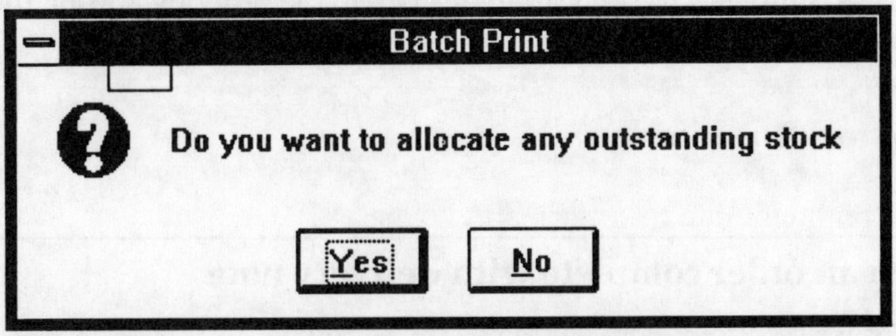

4 CLICK the **No** button to return to the **Sales Order Processing** window.
PRESS [Esc] to return to the **Financial Controller** window.

Task 26 Despatching an order and updating the stock

➤ **In this Task you will learn how to use the Sales Order Processing facility to complete an order.**

Having entered a sales order into the system and having allocated stock to it and produced the delivery note to accompany the order we must now despatch the order. Here the accounting procedure follows the physical procedure. The despatch process completes the allocation of stock to the order by adding the stock to the order and subtracting it from the stock held.

Activity 26.1 To despatch an order complete with delivery note

1 ENSURE that the **Financial Controller** window is being displayed.

2 CLICK the **Sales Order Processing** button to display the two orders currently in the system.

3 CLICK the description of the SMITH order to highlight it and thereby select it.

4 CLICK the **Deliveries** button to reveal the **Sales Order [Enquiries/Deliveries]** window.

5 CLICK the **Complete** button in the **Amend Despatch** box to reveal the **Amend Despatch** window asking you if you wish to fully despatch ALL allocated items.

6 CLICK the **Yes** button and the **Despatch Stock** window appears.

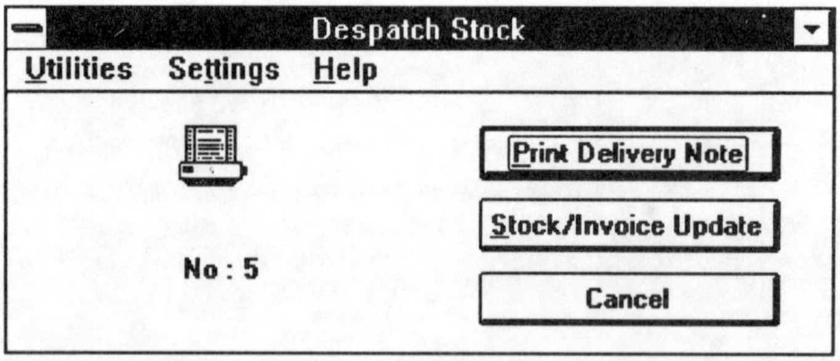

7 CLICK the **Print Delivery Note** button to print the delivery note.

8 When the delivery note has been printed CLICK the **Stock/Invoice Update** button to update the stock record and the ledgers.

When the updating of the stock and ledgers is completed you are returned to the **Sales Order [Enquiries/Deliveries]** window where you will see that the order has been despatched with no further stock allocated or to be despatched.

9 CLICK the **Done** button to return to the **Sales Order Processing** window where the order **Status** is now given as **COMPLETE** to indicate that the processing of this order is now complete.

10 PRESS Esc to return to the **Financial Controller** window.

Activity 26.2 Despatching the LEE sales order

Repeat the procedure of the previous Activity to despatch the LEE sales order. When you attempt to completely allocate from stock, a warning window appears telling you that there is insufficient stock to completely allocate this order. CLICK the **Ok** button to close this warning window and you will see that only 70 of the 80 dozen scallops have been allocated. In addition, when the order is viewed in the information panel of the **Sales Order Processing** window the **Status** is given as **PART**.

Despite the fact that the order is only partially fulfilled, complete the despatch and print the despatch note.

Activity 26.3 Checking the stock levels

1 From the **Financial Controller** window CLICK the **Products** button and review the state of the stock.

You will see that the oysters and scallops have been reduced by the amount necessary to fulfil the SMITH order and the partially filled LEE order.

Task 27

Producing the invoice and updating the ledgers

➤ **In this Task you will learn how to produce all the necessary documentation that is associated with the despatch of goods.**

The sales order to SMITH has been fully allocated from stock and despatched.

Activity 27.1 Printing the invoice

1 ENSURE that the **Financial Controller** window is being displayed and CLICK the **Invoicing** button.

2 CLICK the SMITH account in the information panel and then CLICK the **Stock** button.

A **Warning** window appears telling you that the invoice was created from a sales order and any amendments made will not affect the stock levels.

3 CLICK the **Ok** button in the **Warning** window to reveal the required invoice completed automatically during the processing of the sales order.

The invoice now has the default date.

4 CHANGE the Date to **14/08/XX.**

5 PRINT this invoice and, during the printing, a second **Invoice Printing** window appears.

6 CLICK the **Update** button to reveal the **Update Ledgers** window.

7 CLICK the **Printer** radio button in the **Output** box.

8 CLICK the **Ok** button.

You are returned to the **Invoice** window containing a blank form.

9 PRESS Esc to return to the **Customer Invoice** window where you will see that the SMITH invoice is indicated as having been both printed and posted.

10 REPEAT this procedure to print the invoice and post the details of the partially filled LEE order.

11 When the sales order processing is complete return to the **Financial Controller** window.

Task 28 Viewing the stock

➤ **In this Task you will review the stock viewing facility.**

Having made a number of sales you need to know how much stock you have left to discover whether you need to purchase more to enable you to make further sales.

Activity 28.1 Viewing the stock

From the **Financial Controller** window:

1 CLICK the **Products** button and review the stock details.

You will find from the timber stock details that you only have 3 tonnes left. This is below the re-order level of 5 tonnes so you make a note to place an order with T Feller for another 25 tonnes of cut timber.

You only have 2500 oysters left and you decide to hold off from purchasing any more for the moment as this figure is larger than the re-order level of 1000 oysters.

You have no scallops in stock so you decide to re-order 200 dozen.

This you will do in the next Task.

2 PRESS Esc twice in succession to return to the **Financial Controller** window.

Task 29 Processing a purchase order

➤ **In this Task you will learn how to use the Purchase Order Processing facility.**

The **Purchase Order Processing** facility operates in just the same way as the **Sales Order Processing** facility with the exception that the purchase invoice is not automatically created. The purchase invoice must be entered and processed separately.

Activity 29.1 Entering a purchase order

1 From the **Financial Controller** window CLICK the **P.O.P** (Purchase Order Processing) button to display the **Purchase Order Processing** window.

2 CLICK the **Create** button and ENTER and POST the following two purchase orders into the **Create Purchase Order** window:

100 dozen scallops from HISEA @ £6.00 on a purchase order dated 21/08/94

100 dozen scallops from SMILE @ £5.75 on a purchase order dated 22/08/94

Note: The price of £5.75 is entered into the **Product Item Line** window by changing the default price of £6.00.

The order header and footer details need not be amended from their default values.

3 When the orders are completely entered, **Batch** them for further processing at a later time. ENSURE that you finish with the **Purchase Order Processing** window on display.

Activity 29.2 Processing a purchase order

1 CLICK the **HISEA** order in the information panel of the **Purchase Order Processing** window to highlight the HISEA purchase order.

2 CLICK the **Print Batch** button to reveal the **Batch Print** window asking if you want to put any outstanding stock on order.

3 CLICK the **Yes** button.

4 SELECT the **HISEA** order in the information panel of the **Purchase Order Processing** window and then CLICK the **Deliveries** button to display the first of the two previously created purchase orders.

5 CLICK the **Complete** button to complete the process and update the stock and ledgers and a **Warning** window opens:

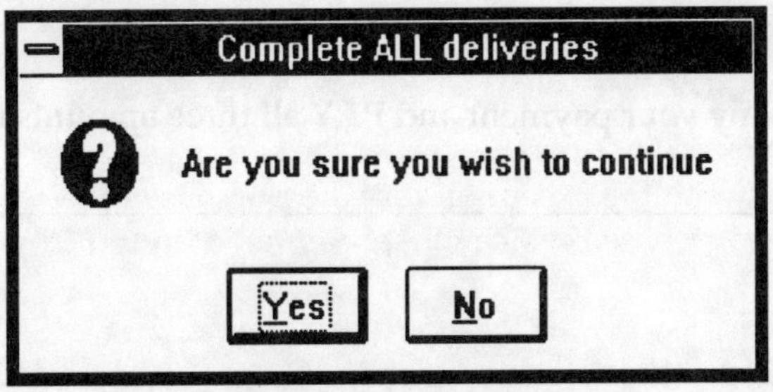

6 CLICK the **Yes** button in this window and then CLICK the **Save** button in the **Purchase Order [Enquiries/Deliveries]** window.

You are returned to the **Purchase Order Processing** window where you will see that the HISEA order now has the **Status** of **COMPLETE** to indicate that the order has been received and entered into stock.

7 When you have completed this process return to the **Financial Controller** window and CLICK the **Products** button. From the **Products** window CLICK the **Swap** button and then CLICK the **Record** button to see for yourself that the stock has been posted.

8 REPEAT this procedure for the SMILE order.

Activity 29.3 Processing the purchase invoice and payment

During the **Purchase Order Processing** the stock was automatically updated but the account ledgers were not. These cannot be updated until the purchase invoice arrives from your supplier which will contain details of which you are unaware, such as Invoice number, for example.

Both invoices have now arrived and so now they must be entered and posted to the ledgers using the additional information:

HISEA Invoice number is 3235 and the SMILE Invoice number is 106.

Both invoices relate to Nominal Code **1001** for stock, Department number **2** and carry a zero rate of VAT. In addition, The HISEA purchase invoice has arrived with a demand to settle all outstanding debts.

1 ENTER and SAVE the two purchase invoices.

2 From the **Financial Controller** window CLICK the **Bank** button to reveal the **Bank Accounts** window.

3 CLICK the **Supplier** button.

4 In the **Pay to** box ENTER the name HISEA (use the **Finder**) and the details of this last purchase order, a previous order and the opening balance appear.

5 ENTER the Date as 24/08/XX and the cheque number as 4.

6 PRINT a remittance advice note to accompany your payment and PAY all three amounts in full.

Activity 29.4 Posting a further purchase invoice payment

You have no credit arrangements with the SMILE account so the delivery was paid for COD with cheque number 5. Post this payment into the ledgers.

Activity 29.5 Completing a sales order

The remainder of a part filled order still exists from a previous Task; the sales order for the LEE account could not be fully allocated. Return to the **Sales Order Processing** facility and complete the order by allocating stock, despatching it, printing all the necessary documentation and updating the stock and ledgers.

Section D

Ending the month's accounting

Task 30 Completing the first month's trading

➤ **In this Task you will reinforce and test your ability to post sale transactions.**

You have completed your first month's trading since your expansion and now is the time to reconcile all your accounts for the month. In this Section you will learn how to produce all the necessary month end reports and how to complete the month's accounting.

By way of a review you will now be required to post sale and purchase transactions to the appropriate ledgers using the **Sales and Purchase Order Processing** facilities.

Activity 30.1 Processing purchase orders

As the month has progressed you have found trade to be quite brisk and as a consequence you have had to make a number of further purchases to satisfy your customer's needs. The following are the details of the purchase orders to be entered into the system:

50 dozen scallops at £6.00 per dozen from HISEA delivered with invoice number 3240, dated 23/08/XX.

100 dozen scallops at £5.45 per dozen from SMILE delivered with invoice number 109, dated 23/08/XX and paid for COD with cheque number 5.

3000 oysters at 25p each from WILL delivered with invoice number 2802, dated 24/08/XX and paid for COD with cheque number 6.

2000 oysters at 27p each from ABC delivered with invoice number 301, dated 25/08/XX.

25 tonnes timber from WOOD at £15 per tonne delivered with invoice number 136, dated 28/08/XX.

They all relate to Nominal Code 1001 for stock and they are all but the WOOD order zero rated for VAT.

1 From the **Financial Controller** window CLICK the **Purchase Order Processing** button.

2 ENTER and PROCESS these purchase orders, invoices and the payments made for COD.

Activity 30.2 Processing sales orders

To match the purchasing activity a number of sales have been made. The details of the sales are as follows:

125 dozen scallops to BLUE despatched 23/08/XX paid for COD.

10 dozen scallops to JONES despatched 24/08/XX.

125 dozen scallops and 100 oysters to OACH despatched 29/08/XX.

1500 oysters to LEE despatched 30/08/XX.

1 From the **Financial Controller** window CLICK the **Sales Order Processing** button.

2 ENTER and PROCESS these sales orders, invoices and the payment made for COD.

Task 31 Periodic procedures

➤ **In this Task you will review the standard reporting facilities that are available within the system.**

Throughout the course of a month's accounting it may be desired to obtain detailed information regarding the state of the accounts. Here we shall review those standard reporting facilities that we have not so far discussed. Whilst it is possible to view all of these reports on the screen you will attain a far clearer view of the state of affairs if you produce a printed copy for each report.

Activity 31.1 Viewing the account balances

Viewing the account balances can give a list of your current liquidity. It can list the current balance of your bank account, money owing to creditors and money owed by debtors.

1 From the **Financial Controller** window CLICK the **Nominal** button.

2 From the **Nominal Ledger** window CLICK the **Report** button to reveal the **Nominal Ledger Reports** window.

3 In the information panel, CLICK each of the following to highlight their descriptions thereby selecting them:

1001 Stock
1100 Debtors Control Account
1200 Bank Current Account
2100 Creditors Control Account

4 CLICK the report **Balances** in the **Files** box.

5 CLICK the **Display** radio button in the **Output** box to ensure the report is sent to the monitor screen.

6 CLICK the **Run** button and the following display results:

N/C	Account Name	Debit	Credit
1001	Stock		421.25
1100	Debtors Control Aaccount	9839.18	
1200	Bank Current Account	776.96	
2100	Creditors Control Account		1877.11

This is showing that the cash you have in the bank is not sufficient to pay your creditors. However, you debtors owe you a substantial sum and if you can get some of that paid in then you could easily settle your debts. You also have a reasonable amount of money tied up in stock.

5 DOUBLE CLICK the **Control-menu** box to return to the **Nominal Ledger Reports** window.

6 PRESS [Esc] twice to return to the **Financial Controller** window.

Activity 31.2 Viewing the Address List

There will undoubtedly be times when you wish to have sight of your customer or supplier list. The customer list can be viewed from the Customers option in the Financial Controller window.

1 From the **Financial Controller** window CLICK the **Customers** button.

2 CLICK the **Report** button to reveal the **Customer Reports** window.

3 CLICK the report **Customer List** in the **Files** box.

4 CLICK the **Display** radio button in the **Output** box.

5 CLICK the **Run** button to produce a screen display of the customer names and addresses.

6 REPEAT the above procedure to produce a printed list of customer names and addresses.

Task 32 Backing up and restoring data

➤ **In this Task you will learn how to back up your data files from the hard disk to a floppy disk**

It is most important that the information stored in your data files on the hard disk is not lost and to maintain safe storage of your data you must back up the data files whenever you leave the Sage Sterling+2 system. It is also advisable to back up your data files prior to executing the month end procedures.

For this Task ensure that you have a formatted floppy diskette available that contains no data, which should be dated and labelled BACKUP.

Activity 32.1 Backing up the data files

1 PLACE your formatted floppy disk in the external drive A.

2 From the **Financial Controller** window CLICK the **Data** menu on the **Menu bar** to reveal a drop-down menu.

3 CLICK the **Backup/Restore** option from the drop-down menu.

4 In the **Directories** box CLICK the symbol **[-a-]** to highlight it and thereby select drive A.

5 CLICK the **Backup** button to reveal the **Backup** window which displays a warning.

6 CLICK the **Yes** button and the backup procedure begins to copy the data files from the hard disk to the floppy disk. Notice, the data files on the hard disk are not affected by this procedure in any way - they are merely copied.

7 When the backup procedure has been successfully completed you are so informed.

8 CLICK the **Ok** button and you are returned to the **Financial Controller** window.
Note: When you attempt to leave Sage Sterling +2 you are always prompted to backup your data. It is a good idea to develop the habit of backing up your data every time you leave the Sage system and the procedure is completely analogous to that described here.

9 EXTRACT your disk from drive A, label it as being a backup disk and annotate it with the current date.

Activity 32.2 Restoring the data files

If, for any reason, you find that your data files on the hard disk have become corrupted since you last backed up your data then you can abandon all the entries that you have made into the system since the last backup and restore the data files to the condition they were in when you last backed up.

1 PLACE your formatted floppy disk containing the last backup in the external drive A.

2 From the **Financial Controller** window CLICK the **Data** menu in the **Menu bar** to reveal a drop-down menu.

3 CLICK the **Backup/Restore** option to reveal the **Backup/Restore Routine** window.

4 In the **Directories** box CLICK the symbol **[-a-]** to highlight it and thereby select drive A.

5 CLICK the **Restore** button to reveal the **Restore** window which displays a **Warning** window.

6 CLICK the **Yes** button in the **Warning** window and the restore procedure begins to copy the data files from the floppy disk to the hard disk.

7 When the restore procedure has been successfully completed you are so informed.

8 CLICK the **Ok** button and you are returned to the **Financial Controller** window.

Task 33 Ending the month

➤ **In this Task you will learn how to complete a month's accounting.**

When the accounting month comes to an end all the ledgers must be balanced and reconciled with each other. This means, amongst other things, that all the prepayments and accruals must be posted, all the recurring entries must be posted, all the asset depreciations must be posted. Fortunately, all these procedures are performed automatically by the Sage Sterling +2 Accounting system.

Activity 33.1 Posting the month's recurring entries

1 From the **Financial Controller** window CLICK the **Bank** button.

2 CLICK the **Recurring** button.

3 CLICK the **Process** button.
This routine will post all the transactions specified in the list of recurring transactions as new transactions on the existing audit trail.

4 When the posting is complete you are returned to the **Bank Accounts** window.

5 PRESS Esc to return to the **Financial Controller** window.

Activity 33.2 Preparing to post monthly entries

1 Ensure that the **Financial Controller** window is being displayed and CLICK the **Period End** button to reveal the **Period End** window.

2 CLICK the **Month End** button to display the **Month End** window.

When you entered prepayments and accruals and depreciation earlier in the Guide the monthly amounts were not posted automatically. Instead their posting into the ledgers has to be initiated by you. This is where you do that.

Activity 33.3 Posting the month's prepayments and depreciation

1 CLICK the **Post Prepayments** and the **Post Depreciation** boxes.

2 CHANGE the date display to **01/09/XX.**

3 CLICK the **Ok** button and the prepayments and depreciation amounts will be posted to the ledgers.

4 When the posting is complete you are returned to the **Month End** window.

5 PRESS Esc to return to the **Financial Controller** window.

Activity 33.4 To check the postings

1 From the **Financial Controller** window CLICK the **Nominal** button.

2 From the **Nominal Ledger** window CLICK the **Report** button.

3 HIGHLIGHT accounts:

1103 Prepayments
8000 Depreciation

4 CLICK the **Activity** report in the **Files** box.

5 CLICK the **Display** radio button in the **Output** box.

6 CLICK the **Run** button.

You will notice that the depreciation in account 8000 is the sum of the two depreciations in accounts 0021 and 0051.

Activity 33.5 Bank reconciliation

When you receive your bank statement from the bank there may be a number of debits and credits relating to transactions executed by the bank that are not reflected in your accounts. For example, the exact value of any bank charges levied by the bank on your account may not be known by you until you receive your bank statement. To ensure that your accounts are a true reflection of all transactions incurred in the name of Erin Fish Supplies you must reconcile your bank statement with your bank account as maintained by the Sage Sterling+2 system.

1 From the **Financial Controller** window CLICK the **Bank** button to reveal the **Bank Accounts** window.

2 CLICK the **Reconcile** button to reveal the **Bank Reconciliation - Bank Current Account** window.

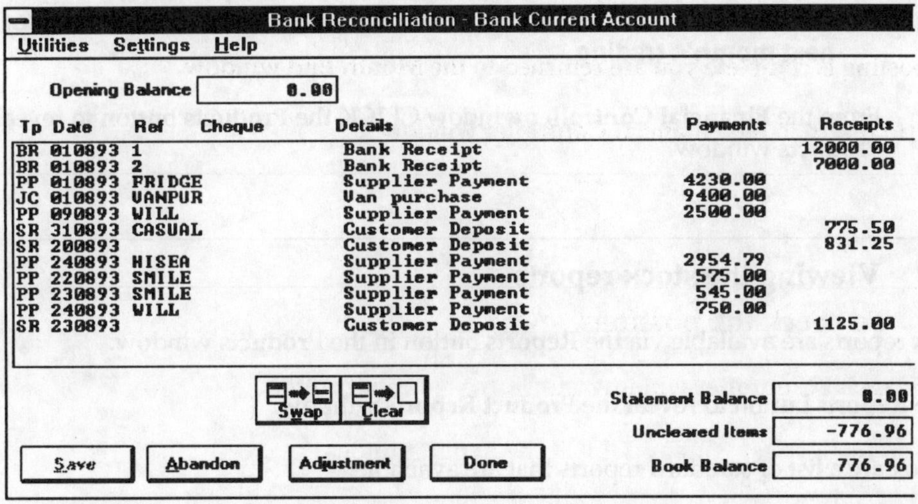

3 CLICK the **Adjustment** button to reveal the **Adjustment** window.

The bank has debited your account in the amount £54.61 for bank charges, this must now be entered into your account as a credit.

4 ENTER the A/C as **7901 - Bank Charges (Use the Finder).**

5 ENTER the Date as **31/08/XX.**

6 ENTER Details as **August bank charges.**

7 ENTER Payment (-) as **54.61.**

8 CLICK the **Save** button.

When the **Adjustment** window closes you will see that this payment is displayed in the information panel.

9 PRESS Esc twice to return to the **Financial Controller** window.

Task 34 Stock reports

➤ **In this Task you will learn how to obtain stock reports and how to reset the stock levels at the end of an accounting month in readiness for the next month's trading.**

From the **Financial Controller** window CLICK the **Products** button to reveal the **Products** window.

Activity 34.1 Viewing the stock reports

Various stock reports are available via the **Reports** button in the **Products** window.

1 CLICK the **Reports** button to reveal the **Product Reports** window.

In the **Files** box are a list of standard reports that are available:

Details
Explosion
Movements
Price List
Products
Profit-Month
Profit-Year
Reorder Levels
Stock History
Valuation

We are interested primarily in four of these reports:

Stock History report
This report displays all the stock movements for each stock item in the report.

Valuation report
This report lists the quantities, values and anticipated monthly sales of each item in stock. The Stock Valuation report is best printed as it is too wide and detailed to view easily on the screen. You will find your timber is valued at £420.00 and your fish at £1951.00.

Profit-Month/Year reports
These reports lists the profit and percentage profit of each item that has sold either during the Month or during the Year to Date. The profit on your fish is £1678.75. The profit on your timber is not recorded because the timber sale used a manual update of the ledgers.

Reorder Levels report
The Reorder Levels report will display details of the quantities of all the stock items alongside their reorder levels.

2 DISPLAY each of these reports on the monitor screen.

3 PRINT out a hard copy of each of these reports.

4 RETURN to the **Financial Controller** window.

Task 35 Ledger reports

➤ **In this Task you will produce reports that are pertinent to the current state of the Sales, Purchase and Nominal Ledgers.**

From the **Financial Controller** window CLICK the **Customers** button to reveal the **Customers** window.

Activity 35.1 The Sales Ledger account balances

The names of the **Sales Ledger** accounts are displayed in the information panel alongside their respective balances. From your screen you will find that there are non-zero balances against four names:

JONES at 2136.94
LEE at 1245.00
OACH at 4958.14
SMITH at 1500.00

To obtain more detailed information about these and other sales accounts a report is necessary.

Activity 35.2 The Sales Ledger transaction history report

1 From the **Customers** window CLICK the **Reports** button to reveal the **Customers Reports** window.

2 PRINT the **Activity** report.

You will be presented with a report entitled **Transaction History** which lists the transaction history of each customer, including:

All invoices issued and all receipts received
Amount Outstanding
Amount paid this period
Credit Limit
Sales Year to Date

Activity 35.3 The Sales Ledger Aged Debtors Analysis

1 When the **Activity** report is complete PRINT a **Balances** report.

You will be presented with a report entitled **Aged Debtors Analysis,** listing each customer.

2 When the printing is complete PRESS [Esc] twice in succession to return to the **Financial Controller** window.

Activity 35.4 The Purchase Ledger account balances

1 From the **Financial Controller** window CLICK the **Suppliers** button to reveal the **Suppliers** window.

The names of the **Purchase Ledger** accounts are displayed in the information panel alongside their respective balances. From your screen you will find that there are non-zero balances against three names:

ABC at	540.00
HISEA at	300.00
WOOD at	1037.11

To obtain more detailed information about these and other purchase accounts a report is necessary.

Activity 35.5 The Purchase Ledger transaction history report

1 From the **Suppliers** window CLICK the **Reports** button to reveal the **Suppliers Reports** window.

2 PRINT the **Activity** report.

You will be presented with a report entitled **Transaction History** which lists the transaction history of each supplier, including:

All invoices received and all payments made
Amount Outstanding
Amount paid this period
Credit Limit
Purchases Year to Date

Activity 35.6 The Purchase Ledger Aged Creditors Analysis

1 When the **Activity** report is complete PRINT a **Balances** report.

You will be presented with a report entitled **Aged Creditors Analysis**, listing each supplier.

2 When the printing is complete PRESS Esc twice in succession to return to the **Financial Controller** window.

Activity 35.7 The Nominal Ledger account balances

1 From the **Financial Controller** window CLICK the **Nominal** button to reveal the **Nominal Ledger** window.

The names of the **Nominal Ledger** accounts are displayed in the information panel alongside their respective debits or credits. To obtain more detailed information about these and other purchase accounts a report is necessary.

Activity 35.8 The Nominal Ledger transaction history report

1 From the **Nominal Ledger** window CLICK the **Reports** button to reveal the **Nominal Ledger Reports** window.

2 PRINT the **Activity** report.

You will be presented with a report entitled **Transaction History** which lists the transaction history of each nominal account, showing the respective debits and credits for each transaction culminating in a total and a debit or credit balance.

Activity 35.9 The Nominal Ledger balances

1 When the **Activity** report is complete PRINT a **Balances** report.

You will be presented with a report entitled **Nominal Ledger Account Balances Analysis,** listing the appropriate debit or credit balances for each nominal account.

2 When the printing is complete PRESS Esc twice in succession to return to the **Financial Controller** window.

Task 36 The Disk Doctor

➤ **In this Task you will learn how to access the Disk Doctor.**

The **Disk Doctor** is a program that permits you to check on the integrity of your data files. The program does not run in the **Windows** environment and so must be run from **DOS**.

Activity 36.1 Accessing the Disk Doctor

1 EXIT from the Sage Sterling+2 system to a display of the two icons *Sterling* and *Doctor* in the **Sage** window in **Windows**.

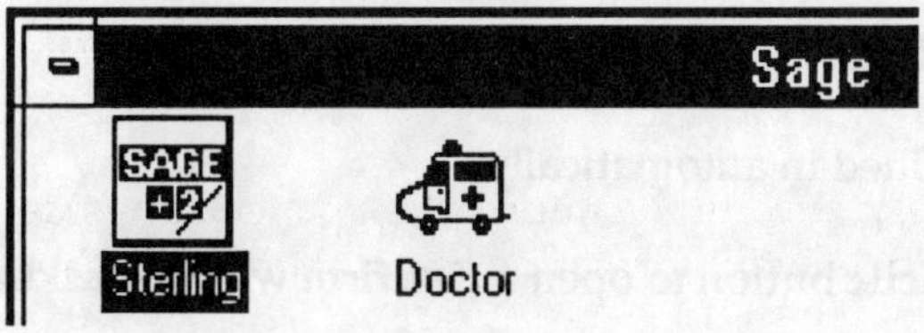

2 DOUBLE CLICK the **Doctor** icon.

In a few moments the screen changes from the familiar graphical display of **Windows** to the text display of **DOS** and the **Disk Doctor** program screen comes into view.

3 CLICK the **Check Data Files** box and the data is checked, during which time the number of Errors, Warnings and Comments are counted on screen as they are found.

When this process is complete the specific errors, warnings and comments can be viewed by clicking the **View Errors, View Warnings** and **View Comments** buttons respectively. However, this Guide is not an appropriate place to discuss structural error correction. For further information REFER to the Sage Sterling +2 User guide.

Correcting ledger entries

Whilst it is not appropriate to discuss structural error correction in this Guide it is appropriate to mention how you can correct minor entry errors such as incorrect dates on invoices which can cause erroneous reports to be produced. From the **Disk Doctor** screen CLICK the **Error Correction** button to open the **Posting Error Correction** window where you will see every single entered transaction listed. Any particular transaction can be selected by moving the highlight using the keyboard up and down arrow keys and then clicking the **Edit** button thereby opening an **Edit Transaction** window. The transaction can then be edited at will and a return to the **Sage** window of **Windows** effected by clicking the **Ok** button, followed by the **Done** button and the **Exit** button.

Task 37 The VAT return analysis

➤ **In this Task you will learn how to generate the details necessary to complete your VAT return.**

From the **Financial Controller** window CLICK the **Financials** button to reveal the **Financials** window.

Activity 37.1 The VAT return

1 CLICK the **VAT Return** button to reveal the **Value Added Tax Return** window in which is displayed an unfilled tax form.

2 ENTER the **Period from** as **01/08/XX** and the **Period to** as **31/08/XX.**

3 CLICK the **Calculate** button and the form is filled in automatically.

4 When the form is complete CLICK the **Reconcile** button to open a **Confirm** window asking if you wish to *flag* VAT transactions.

If a VAT transaction is flagged it will be automatically excluded from subsequent VAT analyses and a - will appear under the VR column in the appropriate transaction history report.

5 CLICK the **Yes** button.

6 CLICK the **Print** button to reveal the **Print** window.

7 CLICK the **Printer** radio button and PRINT all three available reports: Detailed, Summary and VAT Return.

8 ENSURE that when you complete this Activity the **Financial Controller** window is being displayed.

Task 38 The profit and loss report and balance sheet

➤ **In this Task you will learn how to produce a profit and loss report and a balance sheet.**

From the **Financial Controller** window CLICK the **Financials** button to reveal the **Financials** window.

Activity 38.1 The profit and loss report

1 CLICK the **Profit & Loss** button to reveal the **Profit & Loss** window.

2 ENSURE that the display of the Financial Month reads as 1 - August.

3 ENSURE that the output will be to the printer.

4 CLICK the **Ok** button and the **Profit & Loss** report will be sent to the printer.

Activity 38.2 The balance sheet

1 From the **Financials** window CLICK the **Balance Sheet** button to reveal the **Balance Sheet** window.

2 ENSURE that the display of the Financial Month reads as 1 - August.

3 ENSURE that the output will be to the printer.

4 CLICK the **Ok** button and the balance sheet will be printed showing the financial state of the company under the headings:

Fixed Assets
Current Assets
Current Liabilities
Financed By

for both This Month and the Year to Date.

Task 39 The audit trail

➤ **In this Task you will learn to appreciate the information content of the audit trail.**

The most important report of any accounting system is the audit trail which lists the details of every transaction recorded in the system. In the Sage Sterling+2 Accounting System the audit trail is accessed via the **Reports** button in the **Financial Controller** window.

Activity 39.1 Accessing the audit trail

1 ENSURE that the **Financial Controller** window is being displayed.

2 CLICK the **Reports** button to reveal the **Reports** window:

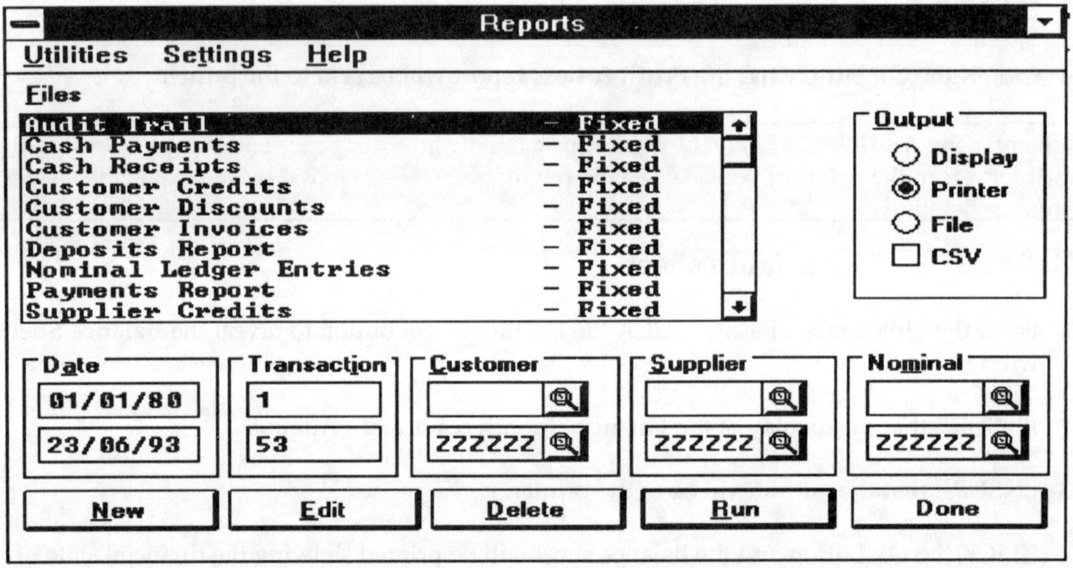

3 HIGHLIGHT the **Audit Trail** report in the information panel and ENSURE that the following is entered in the boxes at the bottom of the window:

	From	To	
Transactions	1	26	Automatically entered
Date	01/01/80	31/08/XX	
Customer	BLUE	SMITH	Use the Finder
Supplier	ABC	WOOD	Use the Finder
Nominal	0010	9999	Use the Finder

4 DISPLAY the **Audit Trail** report on your monitor screen.

As you will appreciate from reading the audit trail, each item describes the point of entry of each posting into the system and its eventual location in the **Nominal Ledger**. For example, the first audit trail entry is the bank receipt of the formation capital. Here the transaction was recorded as a debit into the **Bank Current Account** in the **Bank Control Account** number 1200. This was then automatically entered as a credit in the **Nominal Account** 3102 - Startup Capital.

Only twelve transactions can be viewed at a time.

5 CLICK the slider bar to display further transaction. At the very end of the list you will notice the transactions related to recurring entries, repayments and depreciation.

6 When you are satisfied that you no longer require to view this report DOUBLE CLICK the **Control-menu** box to return to the **Reports** window.

7 RETURN to the **Financial Controller** window.

Activity 39.2 Obtaining a hard copy of the audit trail

Re-enter the **Audit Trail** option of the **Reports** facility and this time send the audit trail to the printer. From the printout you will see the payment details included on the same line as the invoice details.

Task 40 Bespoke reports

➤ **In this Task you will learn how to create new reports to your own design.**

In addition to the predefined reports within the system that you have already met there is a facility for creating new reports to your own design. You have already seen an example of this when you created a list of **Nominal Account** codes in Task 4.

ENSURE that the **Financial Controller** window is being displayed.

Activity 40.1 New Sales Ledger reports

1 CLICK the **Customers** button to reveal the **Customers** window and then CLICK the **Report** button to reveal the **Customer Reports** window.

2 CLICK the **New** button and you will be confronted with the **Customer Report Creation** window containing a list of items that are available for inclusion in a bespoke report:

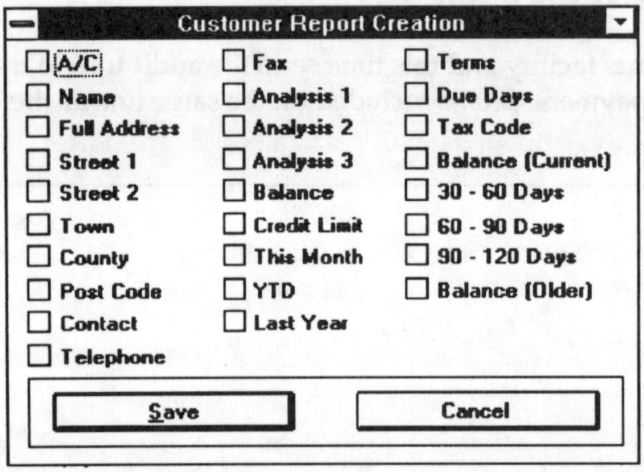

You wish to have a report that you can use at will whenever you wish to call in debts that exceed the credit limits you have set your customers.

3 CLICK the small square box at the side of each of the following items:

A/C	Analysis 1
Name	Credit Limit
Contact	Balance (Current)
Telephone	

As you click each square you will notice that a cross appears to indicate that the item has been selected for the report. If you click a crossed box the cross will disappear, thereby deselecting that item. Try it.

4 When you are satisfied that you have selected all the necessary items CLICK the **Save** button to open a **Save As** window.

5 In the **Save As** window TYPE the Name of the report as **CUSTCRDT** and then CLICK the **Ok** button to save it to the disk under that name.

You will be returned automatically to the **Customer Reports** window where you will see the new report listed in the **Files** box.

6 PRINT the **CUSTCRDT** report and COMPLETE this Activity with the **Financial Controller** on display.

Activity 40.2 New Purchase Ledger reports

1 CLICK the **Suppliers** button to reveal the **Suppliers** window and then CLICK the **Reports** button to reveal the **Supplier Reports** window.

2 CLICK the **New** button and you will be confronted with the **Supplier Report Creation** window containing a list of items that are available for inclusion in a bespoke report:

You wish to glean information from your purchasing history to enable you to convince your suppliers that you are both credit worthy and needful of higher credit limits.

3 CLICK the small square box at the side of each of the following items:

A/C	This Month
Name	YTD (Year To Date)
Contact	Last Year
Telephone	Balance (Current)
Credit Limit	

4 When you are satisfied that you have selected all the necessary items CLICK the **Save** button to open a **Save As** window.

5 In the **Save As** window TYPE the Name of the report as **SUPPCRDT** and then CLICK the **Ok** button to save it to the disk under that name.

You will be returned automatically to the **Customer Reports** window where you will see the new report listed in the **Files** box.

6 PRINT the **SUPPCRDT** report and COMPLETE this Activity with the **Financial Controller** on display.

Task 41 Department reports

➤ **In this Task you will learn how to assign names to departments and how to use the report generator.**

In earlier Tasks we have referred to three departments:

Department 1 - Purchases
Department 2 - Sales
Department 3 - Stock

So far these departments are only numbered within the system. In this Task we shall assign the names to the departments and then create a report that will tell us the values of our purchases, sales and stock.

Activity 41.1 Naming the departments

Access to departmental descriptions can be made via the **Settings menu** on the **Menu bar** that is displayed in a number of alternative windows.

1 From the **Financial Controller** window CLICK the **Customers** button to reveal the **Customers** window.

2 CLICK the **Settings menu** on the **Menu bar** to reveal a drop-down menu.

3 CLICK **Departments** on the drop-down menu to open the **Departments** window.

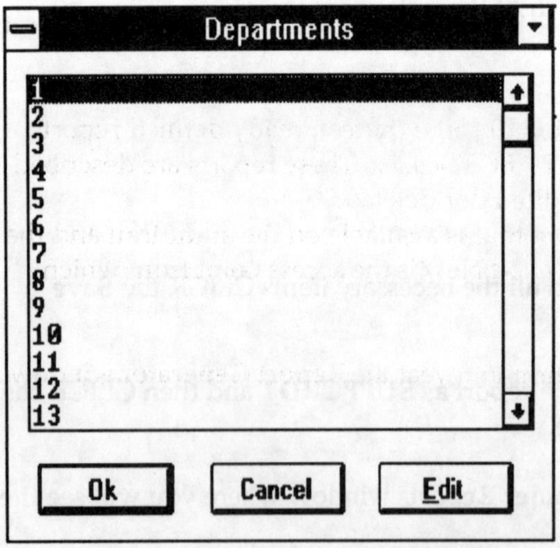

The departments are shown as numbers in the information panel with number 1 highlighted.

4 CLICK the **Edit** button to open the editing window.

5 ENTER the Name of Department 1 as **Purchases** and then CLICK the **Ok** button.

You are returned to the **Departments** window with the name of the first department displayed in the information panel.

6 CLICK the number **2** in the information panel to highlight it and NAME this department **Sales.**

7 NAME the third Department as **Stock.**

8 When you are satisfied that all three departments have their correct names PRESS Esc twice in succession to return to the **Financial Controller** window.

To check that the Department names are now within the system LOOK at the Customer, **Supplier** and **Stock** records where you will see the various departments named in their appropriate locations.

Activity 41.2 The Report Generator window

1 From the **Financial Controller** window CLICK the **Reports** button to display the **Reports** window.

In the information panel you will see a collection of some thirteen ready defined reports ranging from the audit trail through to the VAT - EC sales list. These reports are described as fixed in the sense that they can be neither edited nor deleted.

New reports can be created from information that is available on the audit trail and the button to the right of the information panel labelled **New** is the access point from which bespoke reports can be created.

2 In the **Reports** window CLICK the **New** button to reveal the **Report Generator** window in which is displayed a report definition form:

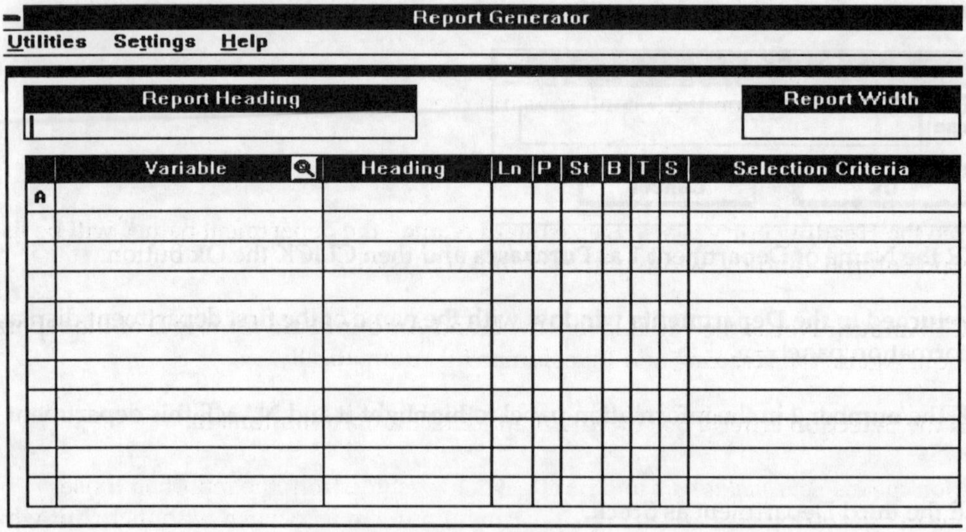

As you will see from the report definition form there are a number of columns under which you can define the particular report you desire. We shall see to what these columns refer in the next Activity when we create a report. What is important to realise at the moment is that the printed report will appear as a collection of *columns*, each column headed by a name - referred to as **Heading**. What appears in a printed *column* is defined by entries in the appropriate *row* of this report definition form.

Activity 41.3 Creating a report

1 ENTER the name of the report as:

Title: **Department Report**

We are going to produce a report that will list all the sales and all the purchases against the appropriate departments.

2 In the first row of the report definition form CLICK the box headed **Variable** and then CLICK the **Finder**.

3 When the **Variable List** window comes into view CLICK the variable **Dept. No.** and then CLICK the **Ok** button.

The phrase **Department No.** is then automatically entered into row A of the column called *Variable* of the report definiton form. In addition, **Dep** appears in the column called *Heading*. This is the heading that will appear on the printed report under which will be listed the account codes. Notice as well that under Ln you will see the number 3. This is the width in number of characters of the printed column.

The **Heading** entry could be amended if you wished to do so but the **Ln** entry cannot be changed.

4 CLICK the **Variable** box on the second row and then CLICK the **Finder**.

5 For the next variable SELECT **Department Name**.

You will see the **Heading** entry is also **Department Name** - the department names will be listed in the second column - and the width of the column (Ln) is 25.

6 SELECT **Amount-Net** as the variable for row C and **Amount Paid** for row D of the report definition. Again, the **Heading** and **Ln** columns fill automatically.

7 CLICK the **Selection criteria** box on row A and ENTER the criterion **!=0.**

This criterion means *not equal to zero* and its effect is to exclude from the report all those transactions in the audit trail that have no department number associated with them but which would appear in the report as department 0 if this criterion were not in force.

8 CLICK the **St** box on row A and ENTER **1A** which will ensure that this column is sorted in ascending order.

9 CLICK the **B** box on row A and ENTER **L**. REPEAT for row B.

This will ensure both a line break between departments and non-repetition of either department name or number.

10 CLICK the **Save** button and save this report to disk under the name **DEPT** after which you are returned to the **Reports** window.

Activity 41.4 Running a report

1 From the **Reports** window CLICK the report **dept** in the information panel to highlight it.

2 CLICK the **Run** button and send the report to the printer.

Section E

The second month

Task 42 Outstanding purchase and sale invoices

➤ **In this Task you will learn how to obtain information from the system that will inform you of all outstanding invoices that either need to be paid to the company or paid by the company.**

Your second month sees a number of problems arise in your trading. You will learn how to make a contra entry, how to deal with a returned cheque and a subsequent bad debt. You will also learn how to account for refunds to customers and refunds from suppliers.

At the commencement of a month's trading you will need to know how much you are owed and by whom. You will also need to know how much and to whom you yourself owe money.

ENSURE that the **Financial Controller** window is being displayed and CLICK the **Reports** button.

Activity 42.1 Viewing outstanding payments via the transaction history

One method of obtaining information regarding outstanding invoices is to consult the transaction histories of both the **Sales** and the **Purchase Ledgers**. When you do this you will find that certain transactions have a star against the value. The star indicates that the invoice is outstanding.

In the **Sales Ledger** the outstanding invoices are:

JONES	2136.04
LEE	1245.00
OACH	4958.14
SMITH	1500.00

and in the **Purchase Ledger** they are:

ABC	540.00
HISEA	300.00
WOOD	1037.11

Activity 42.2 Sales payments

In the light of the information gleaned during the previous Activity you have written to those customers who owe you money and requested immediate payment. All but one have sent you what they owe and have been paid into the bank. These transactions must now be entered into the ledgers.

1 POST the following sales receipts:

JONES	2136.04
LEE	1245.00
OACH	4958.14

2 ENTER the date as **25/09/XX.**

Activity 42.3 Purchase payments

In addition to being paid by your customers you have paid your suppliers the amounts that you owe them. These transactions must now be entered into the ledgers.

1 POST the following purchase payments:

ABC	540.00
HISEA	300.00
WOOD	1037.11

2 ENTER the date as **25/09/XX.**

Activity 42.4 Cash flow

All your customer's bar one have paid you in full and you have paid all your suppliers. You now wish to look at your bank account to see the state of affairs there.

1 From the **Financial Controller** window CLICK the **Nominal** button and from the information panel SELECT **Bank Current Account**.

2 CLICK the **Activity** button to produce a display of every bank transaction that has been made and at the bottom of the screen your bank balance is displayed. A debit of £7184.42. Your cash flow is in order, you have money in the bank.

Task 43 Contra entries

➤ **In this Task you will learn how to make Contra Entries.**

Occasionally one of your company suppliers is also a customer in which case a sale can be offset by a corresponding purchase. In this instance the company has purchased its first month's supply of diesel for the van from the local garage. In the second month the garage owner has asked for a supply of timber and you have agreed to offset the sale by supplying timber to the same value as the diesel fuel purchsed. In this way no cash is transferred between the company and the garage but because the stock level of timber has been reduced the two transactions must be recorded in the accounting system. This is done by posting contra entries.

Activity 43.1 Posting the garage purchase order for diesel fuel

The purchase order details for the first month's diesel fuel arrived during the second month. The details are:

Bayview Garage
Isle of Erin

31 Aug XX

Invoice: 334

To diesel fuel for January:		125.35
	VAT	21.94
	TOTAL	147.29

1 SET UP a supplier account using the Account Reference **BAYP** for the garage and enter the purchase invoice using **Nominal Account** code 7300 for Fuel and Oil.

Activity 43.2 Posting the sale order for timber to the garage

The sale order details for the delivery of timber to the Bayview Garage during the second month are:

To:

Bayview Garage
Ise of Erin 5 Sep XX

Invoice: 11

To timber supply:

5 tonnes at £25.07 per tonne:		125.35
	VAT :	21.94
	TOTAL:	147.29

1 SET UP a customer account using the Account Reference **BAYS** for the garage.

2 When you have done this PRODUCE a sales invoice using the **Invoicing from Stock** facility.

3 PRINT the invoice and UPDATE the ledgers.

Activity 43.3 Posting the contra entries

1 From the **Financial Controller** window CLICK the **Customer** button.

2 CLICK the **Features** menu to reveal a drop-down menu.

3 CLICK **Contra Entries** to reveal the **Contra Entries** window.

4 ENTER the details of the sales and purchase invoices into the **Contra Entries** window using:

Sales A/C **BAYS**
Purchase A/C **BAYP**

All the outstanding sales and purchase invoices are then displayed. In this case there is just one of each.

5 CLICK each transaction, left and right, to highlight them.

6 CLICK the **Ok** button.

7 When the posting is complete PRESS [Esc] to return to the **Financial Controller** window.

Task 44 Credit notes

➤ **In this Task you will learn how to issue a credit note.**

Of the oysters delivered to F Smith some 250 were dead on arrival. The company always undertakes to supply live oysters so you must stand the loss.

Activity 44.1 Issuing a credit note

1 From the **Financial Controller** window CLICK the **Customers** button.

2 From the **Customers** window CLICK the **Credit Note** button to reveal the **Credit Note** window displaying a **Customer Credit Note** form.

3 ENTER the following details into the **Credit Note** form:

A/C	**SMITH**
Date	**15/09/XX**
Ref.	**1**
N/C	**1001**
Description	**Dead stock**
Amount	**1500.00**

The procedure for creating the credit note is the same as that for producing an invoice from stock.

As the tax code for the original transaction was T0 so is the tax code for this credit note. The tax amount is, therefore, zero.

4 When you have completed the posting of this credit note return to the **Customers** window where you will see SMITH still owes £1412.50.

Activity 44.2 Issuing a statement and a credit note

In Task 23 you learnt how to issue statements to customers. Issue a new statement to F Smith and Son Ltd and there you will see the credit displayed.

In Task 20 you learnt how to print an invoice. Repeat this procedure and you will produce the printed credit note.

Task 45 Returned cheques

➤ **In this Task you will learn how to cancel a posted bank receipt.**

Occasionally the company will receive a cheque in payment for a sales invoice for which the customer does not have sufficient funds to meet. In such a case the cheque is *returned to drawer* - your company. If you have already posted this payment through your accounts you will now have to cancel the posting. However, when you do so you will not cancel the tax liability - your company is still liable for the tax that was displayed on the original sales invoice. As a consequence, the next time you issue an invoice to cover the next attempt by your customer to pay the debt, the tax code T9 must be used.

Activity 45.1 Posting a bank receipt

F Smith and Son have responded to the last statement that you sent them and have sent a cheque to the value of £1412.50 by return post. This you immediately paid into the bank.

1 POST the details of the sales receipt.

Activity 45.2 Cancelling the cheque

One week after you had paid Smith's cheque into the bank it is returned to you as *returned to drawer*. You contact Smith by phone and he promises to send another cheque. Meanwhile you must abstract the posted cheque from your accounts.

1 From the **Financial Controller** window CLICK the **Customers** button.

2 From the **Customers** window CLICK the **Features** menu and SELECT **Refunds** to reveal the **Returned Customer Cheques** window.

3 ENTER the following details:

A/C SMITH

The posted cheque appears on the screen, the details highlighted.

4 CLICK the **Save** button to post this cancellation to the ledgers.

5 PRESS Esc twice to return to the **Customers** window screen.

6 VIEW the SMITH account and you will see he still owes £1412.50.

Task 46 Bad debt write-off

➤ **In this Task you will learn how to write off a bad debt from the accounts.**

F Smith and Son Ltd have failed to send the replacement cheque to cover the one that bounced. After repeated attempts to contact the customer you receive the news that they have ceased trading and bankruptcy proceedings are pending. At a creditor's meeting you find out that after all secured debts are covered there will be no money left to cover unsecured debtors such as yourself. As a consequence the outstanding amount owed by F Smith must be written off the books as a bad debt.

Activity 46.1 Writing off a bad debt

1 From the **Customers** window CLICK the **Features** drop-down menu and CLICK **Write off Transactions** to reveal the **Write Off Customer Transactions** window.

2 ENTER the **Maximum Value** for a single transaction as **1500.**
The screen then displays all outstanding amounts owing that are less than or equal to this amount.

3 CLICK the information panel and the SMITH account comes into view.

4 CLICK the **SMITH** account to highlight it.

5 CLICK the **Write Off** button and a **Confirm** window opens asking if **Write Off** does not affect **VAT Write Off Transactions.**

6 CLICK the **Yes** button and you will be returned to the **Customers** window where the SMITH balance now reads as 0.00.

When the account has been written off, a credit note will exist on the system to the value of the amount written off. Also note that the tax liability is not changed - that will have to be a matter between your company and the Customs and Excise.

7 PRESS [Esc] three times to return to the **Financial Controller** window.

Activity 46.2 Viewing the Bad Debt Write Off account

1 From the **Financial Controller** window CLICK the **Nominal** button.

2 From the **Nominal Ledger** window CLICK the slider bar on the information panel until the account **8100 Bad Debt Write Off** comes into view.

3 CLICK the account **8100** to highlight it and then CLICK the **Activity** button to view the effect of writing off the SMITH account.

4 PRESS Esc to return to the **Nominal Ledger** window and then CLICK the **Record** button to view the effect on the budget.

Task 47 Refunding a customer

➤ **In this Task you will learn how to account for a refund to a customer.**

Your delivery to JONES on 24th August last of 10 dozen scallops was found unfit for use some time after they had taken delivery. Your customer reported this fact to you and you agreed to reimburse him. As he was a cash customer he paid COD and he did not want a credit note. Instead he wanted a refund of all the money he had paid on receipt of the goods. From the **Financial Controller** window CLICK the **Customers** button to display the **Customers** window.

Activity 47.1 Refund invoice

1 From the **Customers** window CLICK the **Features** menu and CLICK **Refunds** to reveal the **Customer Refunds** window.

2 ENTER the Account Reference as **JONES** (use the **Finder**).
Three transactions are displayed:

Opening balance	1326.04
Scallops	720.00
Scallops	90.00

3 CLICK the last transaction to highlight it.

4 CLICK the **Refund** button and when the **Confirm** window opens CLICK the **Yes** button.

The transaction is then marked as REFUNDED under **Status**.

5 From the **Customers** window CLICK the **Activity** button to reveal the **Aged Debtors Analysis** window.

6 CLICK the **History** button and in the **Customer Transaction History** window SELECT the JONES account where you will see the refund listed.

7 RETURN to the **Financial Controller** window.

Activity 47.2 Checking the posting

1 CLICK the **Nominal** button and then CLICK **Bank Current Account** in the information panel.

2 CLICK the **Activity** button and there you will find the postings for both SMITH and JONES.

Task 48 Supplier refunds

➤ **In this Task you will learn how to account for a refund from a supplier.**

Your delivery from HISEA on 22nd August last of 50 dozen scallops was found unfit for use some time after you had taken delivery. You reported this fact to your supplier and you agreed that he would reimburse you. As you are a cash customer you paid COD and you did not want a credit note. Instead you wanted a refund of all the money you had paid on receipt of the goods. From the **Financial Controller** window CLICK the **Suppliers** button to display the **Suppliers** window.

Activity 48.1 Refund invoice

1 From the **Suppliers** window CLICK the **Features** drop-down menu and CLICK **Refunds** to reveal the **Supplier Refunds** window.

2 ENTER the Account Reference as **HISEA.**
Four transactions are displayed.

3 CLICK the last transaction to highlight it and then CLICK the **Refund** button.

4 When the **Confirm** window appears CLICK the **Yes** button and the refund will be processed through the ledgers.

5 RETURN to the **Financial Controller** window.

Activity 48.2 Checking the posting

1 From the **Financial Controller** window CLICK the **Bank** button.

2 From the **Bank Accounts** window CLICK the **Reconcile** button where you will see the refund displayed.

3 RETURN to the **Financial Controller** window.

Task 49 Petty cash transactions

➤ **In this Task you will learn how to account for petty cash transactions.**

You are taking a trip to the mainland and you need cash to purchase stationery for the company. This will mean a withdrawal into petty cash and such withdrawals are recorded in the system via a journal entry.

Activity 49.1 Transferring money to petty cash

1 From the **Financial Controller** window CLICK the **Nominal** button and from the **Nominal Ledger** window CLICK the **Journals** button.

Date the transaction as **15/09/XX** and debit the **Petty Cash Account** (account reference **1230**) with 100.00.

2 Credit the withdrawal to the **Bank Current Account** with account reference **1200**.

3 COMPLETE the Activity by returning to the **Financial Controller** window.

Activity 49.2 Processing cash transactions

You have purchased office stationery to the value of £68.50 plus VAT of £11.99 and you now wish to record this transaction.

1 From the **Financial Controller** window CLICK the **Cash** button to reveal the **Cash** window.

2 CLICK the **Payments** button to reveal the **Cash** window displaying a **Cash Payments** form.

3 ENTER the details of the purchase receipt, date 16th September into the **Cash Payment** window using **Nominal Code 7504** for Office Stationery.

Activity 49.3 Transferring money from petty cash to the bank

You have £20.51 change left from the original £100 that you withdrew to purchase stationery. You have put this back into the bank and now you wish to record that transaction. Again it will be a journal entry.

1 **Date the transaction as 17/09/XX and credit the Petty Cash Account (account reference 1230) with 20.51.**

2 **Debit the payment into the bank current account with account reference 1200.**

3 **COMPLETE this Activity and this Guide by returning to the Financial Controller window, leaving the Sage Sterling +2 accounting system and backing up your data.**